A History of the Paper Pattern Industry

The Home Dressmaking Fashion Revolution

JOY SPANABEL EMERY

B L O O M S B U R Y
LONDON · NEW DELHI · NEW YORK · SYDNEY

Bloomsbury Academic

An imprint of Bloomsbury Publishing Plc

50 Bedford Square	1385 Broadway
London	New York
WC1B 3DP	NY 10018
UK	USA

www.bloomsbury.com

Bloomsbury is a registered trade mark of Bloomsbury Publishing Plc

First published 2014

© Joy Spanabel Emery, 2014

British Library Cataloguing-in-Publication Data
A catalogue record for this book is available from the British Library.

ISBN: PB: 978-0-8578-5831-3
HB: 978-0-8578-5830-6
ePDF: 978-1-4725-7745-0
ePub: 978-1-4725-7746-7

Library of Congress Cataloging-in-Publication Data
A catalog record for this book is available from the Library of Congress.

Typeset by Apex CoVantage, LLC, Madison, WI, USA
Printed and bound in India

A History of the Paper Pattern Industry

Contents

List of Illustrations

List of Tables

Acknowledgments

This book is the result of many years of searching though dusty pattern catalogs, fashion magazines, and thousands of patterns. The work was pioneered by Betty Williams, who began laboriously piecing together the history of the numerous pattern companies started in the nineteenth century. She attracted other researchers in her quest, most notably Kevin L. Seligman and me, encouraging us to augment the work she had begun.

A large number of people have contributed to the work in a variety of ways: Kevin Seligman, author, with his expertise on men's tailoring and English pattern companies; from the University of Rhode Island, Sarina Rodrigues, Special Collections, with guidance and support; and Linda Welters and Margaret Ordoñez, Department of Textiles, Fashion Merchandising and Design, with photographic assistance and editorial support. I am grateful as well to Susan Hannel of the Department of Textiles, Fashion Merchandising and Design for taking on the challenge of revising and rendering the patterns in the appendix, and to Claire Shaeffer, freelance author and teacher, for providing important information through her research on pattern company practices over the last forty years. For assistance in obtaining permissions from the pattern companies, I thank Patricia DeSimone of Wilton Brands LLC for Simplicity and Burda and Kathleen Wiktor for McCall, Butterick, Vogue, and Kwik Sew. I am indebted to Roberta Hale, master seamstress, for numerous volunteer hours in the archive and reproductions of small-scale garments from a variety of patterns included in the illustrations. I have special thanks for Whitney Blausen for patiently reading through many versions of the text and challenging me for clarification.

Finally thanks to the editorial team at Bloomsbury: Anna Wright, editor, and Hannah Crump, publishing assistant, for fielding an endless string of e-mails, and Abbie Sharman, editorial assistant, design.

Joy Spanabel Emery
Commercial Pattern Archive
University of Rhode Island
Kingston, Rhode Island

Introduction

Significance

When Western clothing began to reveal the shape of the body in the twelfth century, cloth needed to be cut into shapes and the shapes became more complex in each century, thus requiring guides or patterns to form appropriate shapes to fit the body. The paper pattern ultimately became that guide; however, as Frieda Sorber observed in the exhibition catalog *Patterns* from the MoMu in Antwerp, "The history of the paper pattern is almost as elusive as the ephemeral nature of the object itself" (Heavens 2003: 23).

This book is intended to dispel much of the mystery of the history of patterns and the companies that produced them, with a brief history covering both. The research is based upon publications and tissue patterns primarily from the United States and the United Kingdom. There are numerous cultural facets open for further research and analysis. This introduction is a challenge for further exploration.

It is a fascinating story. The struggles and maneuvers are a microcosm of late nineteenth- and twentieth-century business practices. Beginning with antecedents from the Renaissance with the rise of tailoring, the story traces the history of patterns and the pattern companies from the introduction of dressmaker patterns in the 1840s to the present.

The study of patterns belies two persistent myths about dress patterns. One is the concern about how fragile the patterns are. By and large the tissue paper patterns are not as fragile as they appear primarily because the tissue is usually acid-free paper like that used to wrap fruit (Williams and Emery 1996). Therefore, many patterns have survived, providing excellent historical documentation. Another myth is the concept that the patterns are out of date by the time they reach the customer. Repeated evidence shows that the latest styles were available in a very timely manner. For example, the introduction of Mary Quant's miniskirt in 1965 spurred a bit of a crisis as pattern companies and ready-to-wear retailers alike scrambled to determine where hem length would settle. Pattern companies stayed up to date with the style and met the demand.

With easy and rapid distribution of the latest styles, a skilled needlewoman could aspire to produce the latest styles. With the aid of such fashion magazines as *Godey's*, *Peterson's*, and *Leslie's*, the sewing machine, and greater accessibility to dress patterns by such entrepreneurs as Mme Demorest, Ebenezer Butterick, and James McCall, women could make fashionable as well as serviceable garments. Thus, patterns are credited with the democratization of fashion (Walsh 1979; Paoletti 1980).

Patterns evoke an intimate picture of popular culture and social history, the most immediate being the evolution of fashionable styles primarily for women and children. The styles are for everyday wear. Garments that are saved and preserved in museum collections are primarily high fashion or special occasion garments for an elite few. Patterns provide a detailed, unique record of the evolution of everyday styles from the 1840s to the present. They follow the evolution of fabrics for clothing, revealing the popularity and influence of new synthetics, such as rayon in the 1930s or polyester knits in the 1970s.

Patterns offer an excellent visual resource for defining garment terminology. For example, it is possible to view a nineteenth-century redingote, see the pattern shapes, and compare that to the twentieth-century variations of a redingote. A nineteenth-century sacque can be identified as a woman's jacket for street-wear or intimate undress.

The date of issue for most of the patterns can be determined, which provides an accurate means of dating fashions. Since actual garments rarely come with information as to when they were made, it is very difficult to establish an accurate time frame for a garment. The patterns offer researchers a valuable guide for dating garments, not just by the assessment of the overall style but also by the study and comparison of the shapes of the garment pieces and its construction techniques. The method for dating patterns includes:

- Style of garment,

- Style of pattern company logo,

- Pattern number,

- Price.

In general, the pattern numbers, usually four digits between 1000 and 9999, are recycled. Recycling is not influenced by calendar year; consequently, the lower numbers can overlap higher numbers in the same year. Betty Williams identified several pattern dating specifics in "On the Dating of Tissue Paper Patterns" (1996, 1996–1997). Additionally, some companies use multiple number series to identify different pattern lines. At one point, Vogue had five simultaneous series: regular, special, children, couturier, and Paris Original. Emery (1997–1998) details the complexity of sorting the numbering system in "Dating Vogue Designer Patterns 1958–1988."

Dating patterns produced by syndicates, such as Reader Mail and Famous Features, to be sold by newspapers and specialty periodicals such as farm journals cannot be dated with the above criteria since the pattern styles and numbers were designed to be long-lasting styles useful for several years. Similarly, independent companies often specialize in timeless styles and their patterns are carried in their catalogs for a number of years, making a specific year of issue less relevant.

Betty Williams and the Commercial Pattern Archive

The examination of pattern production was pioneered by Betty Williams, who was passionate about vintage patterns, and she "infected" several of us with her passion. A theatrical costumer, she created costumes for a variety of Broadway and regional theater productions. Period patterns were an invaluable resource for her work on shows set in the nineteenth and twentieth centuries. She became an expert in men's and women's tailoring and the drafting systems so essential for creating authentic men's costumes. For most women's outfits, she looked to the commercially produced patterns from companies such as Butterick, McCall, Simplicity, and Vogue. Initially, she thought the pattern numbers would be sufficient for dating the patterns. She learned quickly that this was not the case. The numbers were sequential but they were recycled regularly. So while the numbers were indeed necessary for ascertaining the year a pattern was issued, there are several other factors in addition to the garment style that need to be identified. These include the company's logo style, envelope design, and price. Betty began to compile a comprehensive list of pattern numbers by year from pattern company catalogs and magazines. On one occasion, I was working with her in the stacks of the Library of Congress (they were still open to the public at that time), collecting the low and high pattern numbers from magazines when we realized that the library had closed while we were working; we were locked in. Fortunately, the Library of Congress is housed in several buildings, all connected by tunnels, and not all the buildings had closed, so we were able to find our way through the maze and leave the building.

The research Betty and her cohorts conducted over a period of several years resulted in a method for dating patterns. She also compiled a supplemental pattern company history. Betty's pattern collection grew during this time; she developed a network of like-minded individuals from around North America who found and donated patterns and related publications.

In 1995, Betty and Jimmy Newcomer, a Fashion Institute of Technology (FIT) faculty member, put together a proposal for an exhibition at the Museum at FIT. The proposal was accepted and *Dreams on Paper: Home Sewing in America* was scheduled to open in 1997. Because Betty's collection had a cut-off date of 1959, Newcomer was to curate the section of the exhibit covering the 1960s to the present. Meanwhile, Betty suffered a recurrence of cancer and was weak but determined. I became her alternate, serving as the consultant for the exhibit, and Whitney Blausen was the exhibit coordinator. Unfortunately, Betty did not live to see the exhibit, but her enthusiasm and spirit were a constant presence.

Throughout her illness, she composed a blueprint for the exhibit and began compiling a history of pattern making including tailoring and commercial patterns. Her papers are a major informant for chapters 1 through 9. Material in each of those chapters has been expanded and augmented as new information has been found. Betty's expansive collection of books, journals, and patterns—now at the University of Rhode Island (URI) libraries—is the cornerstone of the Commercial Pattern Archive. Other collections in the archive include the URI Theatre Department and Joy Spanable Emery collections. Major collection donations include the Butterick Archive, Susan Ward, Linda Sarver, and Elizabeth Brown collections. Patterns in the archive are international, including those from the United States, England, France, Germany, and Spain, creating an international view of everyday wear and allowing the researcher to make valuable comparisons.

The materials in the archive are the major reference resource for this book. The archive has three components:

1 Commercial patterns dating from 1840s to present;[1]

2 Printed matter including sewing manuals, professional journals, fashion periodicals, and pattern trade catalogs;

3 Personal papers and compiled research materials.

The patterns are made specifically for commercial use to be sold to individuals over the counter or by mail order. A digital catalog of the patterns with images of the designs and schematic of the pattern pieces is available in the Commercial Pattern Archive database, CoPA. The URI library catalog, Helin, lists the printed matter, and finding aids for personal papers and research materials are on the URI Library Special Collections home page.

Patterns produced for retail by major companies, detailed in the text, can now generally be dated as to when they were first issued. This data is available in the compiled research materials in the archive and CoPA. Furthermore, the database contains catalogs of other pattern collections in North America and the United Kingdom. These collections include the Kevin L. Seligman collection at the Los Angeles County Museum of Art and the Fashion Museum in Bath, England, among others.[2]

Long considered to be of little significance, patterns have been seen as merely disposable tools, intended primarily for women. Fortunately, this perception is changing as the subject is explored in publications such as *The Culture of Sewing*, *Forties Fashion and the New Look*, Janet Arnold's (1972) *Patterns of Fashion* series, exhibition catalogs such as *Patterns* (2003), and a number of international museum exhibitions. As tools, they are necessary for creating all kinds of clothing from intimate apparel and everyday wear to special occasion garments. A 1916 advertisement in *The Designer* best sums up the impact of dressmaker patterns: "There is nothing so cheap & yet so valuable; so common & yet so little realized; so unappreciated & yet so beneficial as the paper dress pattern. Truly one of the great elemental inventions in the world's history—The Tissue of Dreams" (*Designer*, October: 37).[3]

1

Tailoring and the Birth
of the Published Paper Pattern

The earliest surviving published work on patterns is Juan de Alcega's ([1580] 1979) *Libro de geometria practia y traca* (*Book of the Practice of Tailoring, Measuring and Marking Out*), first published in 1580. In the preface, Alcega states he has accomplished "something quite new and never before seen in Spain." The book's purpose was to instruct tailors on methods of cutting out pattern pieces so as to get the most garment from the least amount of fabric. Since all fabric in the sixteenth century was hand-loomed and very expensive, wasting the least amount was of supreme importance (see Figure 1). The pattern pieces are presented as small diagrams drawn more or less to scale (see Figure 2). Few measurements are given. The book contains pattern layouts for men's and women's garments.

In 1588, another Spaniard, Diego de Freyle, wrote *Geometria y tracia para el oficio de los sastres*. It is similar to Alcega's book in content and layout, as is *Geometria y traca perteneciente al oficio de sastres* by Francisco de la Rocha Burguen (1618) and *Geometria y trazas pertenecientes al oficio de sastres* by Martin de Anduxar (1640). Fashions had changed considerably since 1580 so the shapes of the pattern pieces are appreciably different in each.

The oldest surviving French pattern book is *Le Tailleur Sincere* by Benoit Boullay published in 1671. Francois Alexandre Garasualt, also a Frenchman, authored a multivolume work, *Descriptions des artes et métiers: L'Arte du tailleur* (1769) and *L'arte de lingerie* (1771). Denis Diderot and Jean le Rond D'Alembert's *Encyclopedie* (1776) is a major resource for decorative arts and fashion in the eighteenth century, with a large section devoted to patterns and tailoring.

The Tailor's Complete Guide (1769), "the whole concerted and devised by a Society of Adepts," is the oldest known work on cutting in English. Edward B. Giles, a working tailor and one of the most respected tailoring writers of his time, wrote *The History of the Art of Cutting in England* (1887), in which he summarized his low opinion of the work:

Any method more simple or rudimentary than this one published by "A Society of Adepts" can scarcely be conceived. It is really the result of experience and differed scarcely but in name from the plan of cutting by "rock of eye." It must be regarded as proof that a desire or necessity was felt for some method by which tailors could draft these patterns from measures. In default of any other guide, this work may have been of some assistance to the cutters of that

FIGURE 1 The Tailor *by Jost Amman, ca. 1568. Commercial Pattern Archive.*

time; otherwise it is remarkable that the authors should have felt justified in publishing such a primitive method giving so little aid to students. Its issue could only be warranted by the non-existence of any other published method, and in those circumstances it was better than none at all. (Giles [1887] 1987: 77)

The "rock of eye" method is based on experience with pattern shapes and dimensions for garments (and preexisting pattern in the appropriate size). Using a measure and chalk, a person draws the pattern freehand, mentally calculating a drafting formula. Giles quotes Edward Minister Sr.: "I was put in the business in 1802. There was no such thing as system of cutting in those days; the shape was produced by what was termed the rock of eye system. The eye being a globular and very slippery member, there was no certainty where it would rest" (Giles [1887] 1987: 146).

Although not published until 1809 in Philadelphia, *The Tailor's Instructor* by James Queen and William Lapsley can really be placed at the end of the eighteenth century. Generally considered

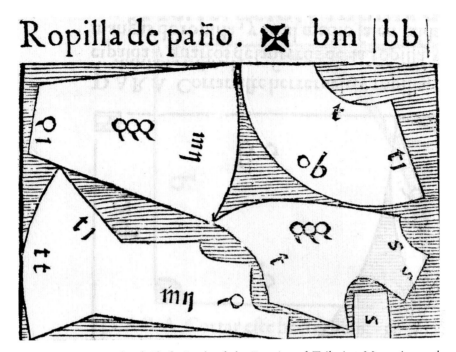

FIGURE 2 *Cassock of Cloth*, Book of the Practice of Tailoring Measuring and Marking Out *(Alcega [1580] 1979: Figure 29a). It is possible to make full-size patterns from the diagrams by laying a graph over the diagram and grading up to full size. Since there are no instructions for scaling up the pattern given in the text, it is not known what method Alcega or the other tailors used. Courtesy of the Crowood Press, Ltd.*

the earliest work on patterns for tailoring published in the United States, it is an almost completely pirated edition of the English book *The Tailor's Complete Guide*.

Publication increased dramatically at the end of the eighteenth century with numerous tailors offering theories, systems, and philosophies of pattern drafting. While there is much overlapping, an enormous amount of information was being offered and the concept of patterns and pattern usage made great strides. Giles's observations of the tailoring profession in 1800 are as follows:

Happy was the tailor who possessed a good fitting pattern: it was cherished by him as a valuable trade secret. In indentures it was sometimes stipulated that the master should give a copy to his apprentice, but was done only on condition of strict secrecy. So precious were these patterns considered they were often bequeathed as a fitting legacy from father to son. (Giles [1887] 1987: 88–89)

Giles further comments on the great value assigned to the patterns, in that tailors referred to the patterns as "Gods," a term occasionally in use today.

By the end of the eighteenth century, there were tailors who were teaching cutting, outside the apprentice systems, to anyone who could pay the fee. In addition to conversations with old tailors, Giles examined circulars from at least one of the teachers of cutting, a Mr. Dietrichstein, and found that he "issued a number of patterns from his establishment on Rathbone Place, which were sold in all parts of England." It appears to have been the custom of country master tailors to go to London to observe and get patterns for the newest fashions. Tailors had to pay a heavy price for Dietrichstein's patterns. A complete set of useful pattern models cost £5, equivalent to $504 in 2010 (Giles [1887] 1987: 91).

Tailors' Pattern Drafting Systems: 1800–1860

Publishing a tailor's treatise with explanations and illustrations of the author's system for drafting patterns was increasingly popular. While these books did not offer completed patterns as such, they purported to give the reader a method for drafting his own patterns. Two drafting systems, or methods, predominated in the early part of the nineteenth century:

1   The proportional scale is a system that relies upon the concept of standard body shapes and relationships. For example, if the chest measurement is X, then the waist is Y and the length of the torso is XX.

2   The direct measurement system relies on the specific, very detailed, set of measurements for a person to achieve an accurate garment.

Many tailors' systems used elements of both.

The authors Cook and Golding developed a proportional scale, which they published in *The Tailor's Assistant* in 1815. They declared that "if strictly attended to, [the system] will enable the practitioner to acquire a degree of certainty of fitting his customers, which is the chief object of the present undertaking" (Cook and Golding 1815: 6). The second edition, published in 1817 and titled *Golding's New Edition of the Tailor's Assistant or Improved Instructor*, offers "accommodation, to acquire a competent knowledge of this system; patterns or models may be had of the author, of every garment, and of any form and fashion, upon a proportionate scale, by sending the particulars of measure" (Golding 1817: 8). In other words, he was selling made-to-order patterns intended for the professional tailor. The volume covers only coats and overcoats. In 1818, Golding published *Part II* for waistcoats and breeches pattern drafts and included the same offer for made-to-order patterns.

In 1818 Mr. Hearn, an English tailor said to be the "first direct measurement tailor in England," published *Rudiments of Cutting Coats*. Giles thought highly of Hearn's work and reprinted large sections of it. In his summary in *The History of the Art of Cutting*, he states, "The claim Mr. Hearn has to our respect and gratitude is founded on the fact that he is probably the first English author to reduce the Art of Cutting to precise rules" (Giles [1887] 1987: 118).

A prolific author, Hearn published works including *Hearn's Table Of Quantities & Positions For Dress Coats, &c. or The Tailor's Ready Assistant* (1819, 2nd ed.); *Hearn's Systematic Method of Cutting Coats, &c. of All Sizes* (1822); *Hearn's Art Of Cutting Ladies' Riding Habits, Pelisses, Gowns, Frocks, &c, Also Ladies' Chaise Or Phaeton Coats, &c., &c.* (1825); and a second edition of *Hearn's Rudiments of Cutting with An Easy Guide To The Use of The Printed Tape Measure*. It is not known when or by whom the "inch measure" was first introduced. The old method of using strips of parchment with appropriate notches for proportions labeled with the customer's name was in practice though the eighteenth century. Hearn extols the superiority of the printed inch measure, which he also sold (see Figure 3).

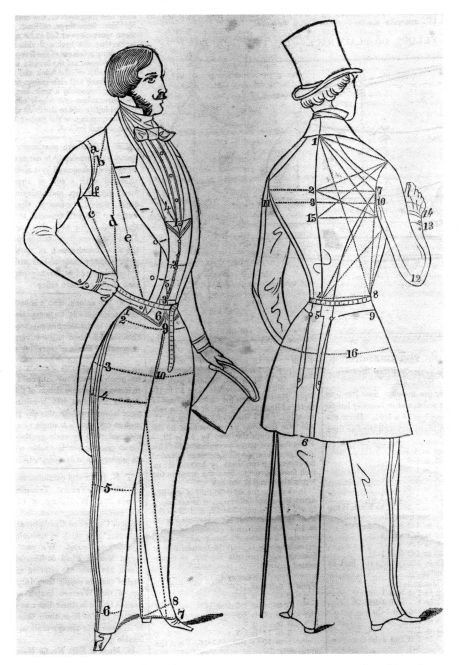

FIGURE 3 *Directions for Taking Measurements.* Scott's Mirror of Fashion *(Scott 1849). Commercial Pattern Archive.*

Tailoring Journals

Louis Devere started the *Gentleman's Magazine of Fashion* in 1828. Intended for tailors, it contained drafts for menswear (see Figure 4). By 1835 Thomas P. Williams & Co. of New York introduced *The Tailor's Magazine* containing drafting systems; it was one of the first American tailoring journals.

Benjamin Read, an entrepreneurial English tailor and printmaker/publisher, began publishing large color fashion plates to sell his wares, which included his "patent measures" (system) around 1829. The large plates featuring a variety of fashions, mostly for men, were offered twice a year for summer fashions and winter fashions. In an advertisement in 1839, Read announced, "The variety of full-size patterns which accompany the prints each season will never be any additional charge" (Read et al. 1984: n.p.). Read was a pioneer in advertising. Apparently, he was the first tailor to issue his own prints. Thus, he developed a procedure for promoting his product that would be widely imitated by others. A few years later, American pattern companies would adopt the practice of publishing their own catalogs and periodicals to promote sales of their products.

Books for tailors containing drafting systems continued to proliferate. (For a comprehensive bibliography of tailoring publications, see Seligman 1996.) Dr. Heinrich Friedrich Wampen published *Wampen's Measures to Construct Models for Gentleman's Dress* in 1841. He was convinced that the art of cutting patterns could be reduced to mathematical (anthropometric) and scientific principles. He became a major influence on the English tailors and pattern makers of the day.

Many tailoring periodicals were being published, all of which included pattern drafts in each issue. In an advertising flyer, Genio Scott, editor and publisher of *Report and Mirror of Fashion*,

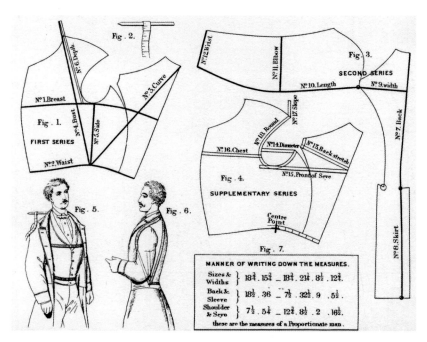

FIGURE 4 *Louis Devere*, Handbook of Practical Cutting on the Centre Point System, *1866, Courtesy of R. L. Shep (Devere [1866] 1986).*

later *Scott's Mirror of Fashion*, boasts that his is the "first attempt in America to establish fashions in dress in America" (1840: n.p.). In London in 1846, Thomas Good started *The Herald of Fashion* to compete with Edward Minister and Sons' *Gazette of Fashion*, which incorporated with *The Tailor & Cutter* in 1950.

Full-size patterns for men's tailored garments were becoming widely available by 1849 (Williams Papers). Williams cites ads for full-size patterns for men's tailored garments in several journals including Minister's *Report of Fashion* and Scott's *Mirror of Fashion*. Available sizes were not mentioned and some patterns were cut to order. A monthly French publication, *The Elegant*, appeared in an English-language edition as early as 1847. In addition to the usual drafting, they also included a full-size pattern with each issue by 1848 (see Figure 5).

Books containing drafting systems continued to proliferate. In London, Edward Minister published a second edition of *The Complete Guide to Practical Cutting* in 1853, Charles Compaing

FIGURE 5 *French Fashion Plate.* The Elegant, *August 1849. Commercial Pattern Archive.*

(Journal des Tailleurs) teamed up with Louis Devere to produce the first of many editions of *The Tailor's Guide* in 1855. In New York, Thomas Oliver published *The Author's Masterpiece* in 1852; Genio Scott published *A Cutters' Guide* in 1857; and T. H. Whitmore published *Whitmore's System* in 1852. Books on pattern drafting were also cropping up in some unlikely places. In 1852 in Glasgow, Kentucky, A. J. Heenter published *The Garment Cutter and Ladies Guide*. In Cincinnati, Ohio, J.C.D. Greve printed *Art Du Tailleur Answeinung zum Zuschneiden*. Cincinnati had a large German population and was a thriving metropolitan city known as the "Gateway to the West."

By the mid-nineteenth century, proportional pattern diagrams begun by Alcega were phased out and replaced by drafting systems to create the appropriate size, and full-size patterns were published. In some instances these were available in a range of sizes.

Tailoring Publications: 1860–1880

Tailoring periodicals, with their monthly drafting of current styles, increased in popularity. Many offered full-sized patterns. *Minister's Gazette of Fashion* had included patterns since the 1840s and continued to do so in their *Monthly Gazette*. By June 1870, Devere's *Gentleman's Magazine of Fashion* was offering full-sized patterns with each issue in addition to its pattern drafts. *The West End Gazette*, begun in 1861, achieved a wide circulation by the 1870s. After a somewhat rocky start in the 1860s, *The Tailor and Cutter* became a respected journal in the following decade.

British publications predominated; however, John J. Mitchell began publishing *The American Fashion Review* in 1874; the publication title was changed to *The American Tailor and Cutter* in 1880. Mitchell offered numerous publications containing pattern drafts, offered to make patterns to the customer's measurements, and supplied ready-made patterns "cut from the finest manila paper . . . for FINE CUSTOM TRADE [emphasis in original] . . . patterns in eleven sizes (Mitchell 1883: 5:1:iii) (see Figure 6). Ebenezer Butterick, a Massachusetts tailor and founder of the Butterick

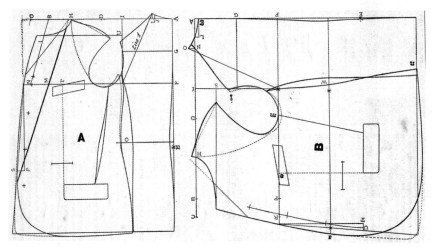

FIGURE 6 *Sack Coat Draft*. The American Tailor, *August 1883. Commercial Pattern Archive.*

Pattern Company, began publishing *The Tailor's Review* in 1866 solely to sell their men's and boys' tissue patterns, but by the 1870s, he was also including pattern drafts and offering ten free patterns with each issue.

Since London was the acknowledged fashion leader in men's wear and set the standards for much of the world's tailoring, it was to be expected that it was also the major publishing center for works of pattern drafting. In 1875, Giles published *The West End System*, which was one of dozens of pattern drafting books circulated by the *West End Gazette* from the 1870s until the First World War.

The John Williamson Company released an endless series of works on pattern drafting. Although the author of the 1879 *Tailor and Cutter Reliable System*s is unknown, the majority of the

BRITISH COSTUMES.—From The Tailor and Cutter.

FIGURE 7 British Costume. *July fashion plate originally published in* The Tailor and Cutter *(London) in July 1883 and then* The American Tailor, *September 1883. Commercial Pattern Archive. The men's sack coat is similar to the* American Tailor *draft.*

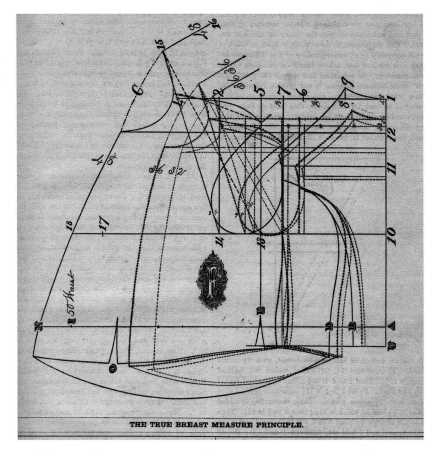

THE TRUE BREAST MEASURE PRINCIPLE.

FIGURE 8 *The True Breast Measure Principle.* The American Tailor, *July 1883.*
Commercial Pattern Archive.

Tailor and Cutter books were written by W.D.F. Vincent. The issues included illustrations of the
latest tailored fashions for men, women, and children. The sack coat in Figure 7 is similar to the
pattern draft in Figure 6. In 1876, Thorton (1899), author of "Tailors of the Century," issued *The Double Shoulder Measure System*, and in 1884, Campaign and Devere published yet another revised
edition of their popular *Complete Manual of Cutting* (see Figures 7 and 8).

Tailoring Publication: 1880–1900

Books on drafting for the tailoring profession continued to proliferate. Charles Hecklinger's *The
Dress and Cloak Cutter* enjoyed considerable popular success in 1877, and *Ladies Cutting Made
Easy* was published in 1885 by T. H. Holding, both representative of the numerous offerings avail-
able to tailors.

Men's wear patterns, known as block or model patterns, were sold though tailoring periodicals.
The use of block patterns, known as slopers in dressmaking terms, had become so prevalent that

the trade journals began writing about them. In a series of articles on "The Art of Cutting by Block Patterns" in the *West End Gazette*, George Wright noted,

A model or block pattern is one that has either been systematically drafted to fit a proportionate figure of a given size, or it may be a correct copy of a garment having the essentials of perfectness both in style and fit whereby they can with confidence be used for all ordinary purposes. We might go further and state how important it is for a man to be able to use block patterns and not only so but also to produce his own, without being dependent upon the production of others, as many are now-a-days. (Wright 1894: 114) (see Figure 9)

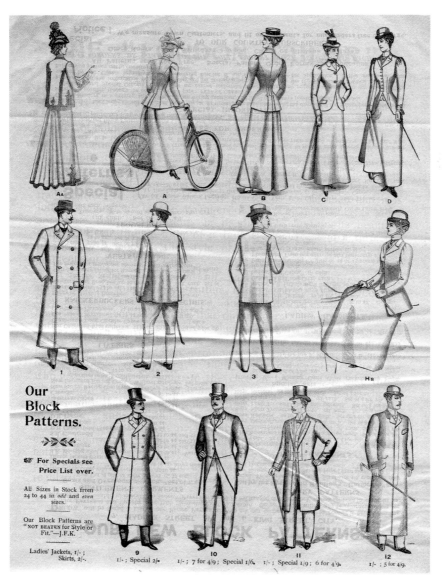

FIGURE 9 *Block Pattern Advertisement, ca. 1897.* Alterations and How to Use Block Patterns, *London: T. H. Holding. Commercial Pattern Archive.*

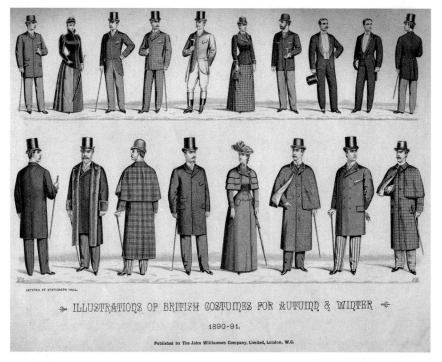

FIGURE 10 Illustrations of British Costumes for Autumn and Winter, *1890*. The Tailor and Cutter, *September 11, 1890. Commercial Pattern Archive.*

Two full pages listing "Stock and Special Patterns, for Gentlemen, Ladies, Juveniles and shirts, in a full range of sizes" appear in the *Cutter's Practical Guide to Ladies' Garments* published in 1892. J. P. Thorton's *The Sectional System of Gentleman's Garment Cutting* published by Minister and Co. in 1893 contains a full page advertising Minister's "Standard and Special Patterns" for gentlemen, ladies, juveniles, military, clerical, and livery, all in a full range of sizes. The three sources mentioned above are all English. However, the sale of men's tailoring patterns was practiced in America as well. The availability of block patterns in several sizes for tailors was firmly established by the 1890s (see Figure 10).

Vincent, undoubtedly the most prolific writer on the subject of pattern drafting, published the *Cutter's Practical Guide* and others between 1870 and the 1920s. By the turn of the century, he discarded his system, which was rather complex (and required the use of a set of graded rulers), in favor of a direct measure system. The new system was clear and straightforward and produced excellent patterns. For many years he was editor of the English journal *Tailor and Cutter*, and when he died in 1926 tailoring journals all over the world ran admiring and respectful obituaries.

Summary

Pattern publications from the sixteenth century through the seventeenth century were written by and for tailors. These Spanish and French publications consisted of small-scale diagrams of

FIGURE 11 Tailor's Workroom, *ca. 1905*. The Art of Measurement, *London: John Williamson Co. Ltd. Commercial Pattern Archive.*

patterns for constructing garments for men and women. By the eighteenth century, English tailors also began publishing how-to journals. All sought solutions for providing the perfect fit for a wide variety of body types. Three major methods for making patterns emerged. The earliest was the rock of eye method, which combined freehand drafting of pattern shapes with measurements. By the early nineteenth century, two drafting systems to create the pattern shape were developed: the proportional and the direct measurement systems. Tailors' patterns were highly valued and protected for fear of theft; however, by the 1850s, tailors gradually began to sell full-size patterns to others in the profession, indicating a distinct shift in proprietary attitudes.

English and American journals for tailors flourished during the last half of the nineteenth century and well into the twentieth. These included drafts of men's and women's tailored garments as well as ads for patterns for sale. The latter were often referred to as block or model patterns and were made available in a range of sizes.

Amid this wealth of tailoring patterns in various forms, the question arises as to who was using what. In the absence of any real information, the answer can only be guessed at. Initially, the tailoring patterns were for professional tailors and, to a certain extent, the emerging ready-to-wear garment industry. Tailors are extremely slow to change their ways, so it seems reasonable to use the tailoring practices of today for hints about the late nineteenth century. Today, over one hundred years later, custom tailors are still drafting each garment directly on the fabric, just as their predecessors would have done (see Figure 11). So it seems safe to say that in the second half of the nineteenth century, most custom tailors were using one of the now numerous variations on drafting systems and making patterns for sale. It is a reasonable guess that the rapidly growing ready-made garment industry was the major purchaser of these patterns, particularly the ones in groups of graded sizes. These patterns were, after all, the new technology of their time.

2

Development of Dressmaking Patterns

1800–1860

Early Publications to the 1830s

Through the eighteenth century, methods for communicating the latest fashions were limited to word of mouth, fashion dolls known as Pandoras, fashion plates such as *Galerie des Modes*, and publications for professional tailors.

Clothing production was the prerogative of male tailors and female dressmakers or mantua makers[1] who produced fashionable dress. The nineteenth century ushered in expanded communication of fashions and clothing construction.

At the end of the eighteenth century, publications with garment patterns for "those desirous of doing good works" appeared. The earliest of these known to have survived is *Instructions for Cutting out Apparel for the Poor* (1789).[2] The book contains thirty large plates and illustrations of the garments. In addition to elementary instructions with precise measurements for various garments that are made from squares and rectangles, there are a few full-size patterns. The patterns for robes, frocks, and caps are mostly for very young children and will therefore fit on the book's foldout pages. Several of the children's garments are shown in graded sizes, the earliest known example of such a practice. There are also patterns for a man's shirt and women's shifts. The instructions are quite puzzling by today's standards, but to women of the 1790s who were familiar with the construction details of the day, they would have been a clear, accurate, and useful source for making garments.

The Ladies' Economical Assistant[3] by "A Lady," published in 1808, contains twenty-seven plates of full-size patterns for babies', children's, and women's garments, shirts for men, and "linen for Lying-in Women." The author recognizes that the patterns are for "several articles of wearing apparel that are not likely to be much affected by fashion."

The pattern pieces in both publications are only for those that make up the basic garments. No patterns are given for facings, pockets, linings, and so forth. The full size is one size only and designated, in some instances, only by age. The assumption is anyone using the patterns would know how to make the garments once they had the main shapes. It was presumed that seamstresses and home sewers had cutting and sewing skills.

Dressmaking Publications: 1830s

The 1830s saw the beginning of what was to become a flood of garment-related books and periodicals for women that contained some form of pattern. Two early English publications, one a handbook and one a fashion periodical, became the guides for future pattern publications. The handbook, *The Workwoman's Guide* by A Lady, published in 1838, was aimed at the same market as the previous books but with expanded content and more-fashionable items. The periodical, *The World of Fashion*, begun in London in 1824, was a monthly magazine featuring the latest fashion news.

    The Workwoman's Guide contained a variety of patterns for the home sewer and "instructions to the inexperienced in cutting out and completing those articles of wearing apparel, etc. which are usually make at home" (1838: iv). The patterns are not full size but presented as scale drawings with measurements and clear instructions. In addition to garments for women and children, it contains patterns for men's garments such as shirts, cravats, and nightshirts. The patterns include a variety of stylish sleeves, bodices, and stays for men and women, as well as caps and bonnets, shoes and slippers, and even upholstery and window draperies (see Figures 12 and 13).

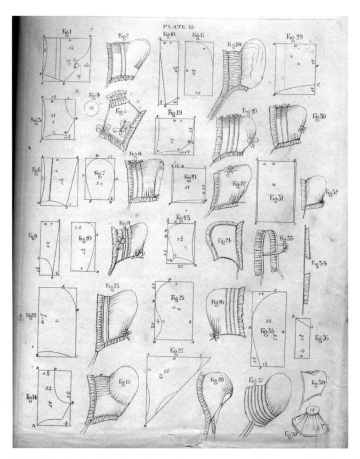

FIGURE 12 *Lady's Day Caps. Workwoman's Guide (1838: plate 15, p125n). Commercial Pattern Archive.*

FIGURE 13 *1830s Day Cap inspired by* Workwoman's Guide. *Courtesy of the University of Rhode Island Theatre Department.*

It is possible that full-size patterns for women's garments were available as early as 1836, but none are known to have survived; however, there is evidence in many of the fashion periodicals of patterns for sale. In the October 1836 edition of the English fashion periodical *The World of Fashion*, a pair of authors, Madame and Mrs. Follet advertised patterns "of every new style of dress exquisitely formed in the exact models and colours in which they were worn, consisting of full length and small size French paper . . . sold at 10s per set [a set included four separate pieces]" (*World of Fashion* 1836: n.p.). It is unclear as to what constituted a set. Adburgham suggests a set may have included separate patterns for a bodice, a basque, collars, and a sleeve (1989: 39–40).

The French publication *Journal des Demoiselles*, issued in 1833, was especially for the home sewer. In its early years it had scaled proportional pattern drafts with sufficient measurements to produce a good pattern. It continued to publish scaled patterns throughout the 1840s and by 1845 was beginning to include a few full-sized patterns, mostly for baby clothes and caps, as pullout inserts in the periodical. Another French magazine, *Petit Courrier des Dames*, was publishing full-size patterns on pattern sheets with the pattern pieces overlaid to fit on the sheet by 1844 (see Figure 14). Frank Leslie used the same approach ten years later in the first volume of *Frank Leslie's Gazette of Fashion*, with the Demorest patterns included as supplements in the periodical (see Figures 15 and 16; see also Appendix 1 for pattern). Additional popular French publications include *Journal Des Modes*, *Moniteur de la Mode*, and *Le Conselier des Dames et Des Demoiselles*.

In all instances, the patterns were a boon to the home seamstress of the time, but to modern eyes they present a number of problems. They come in only one medium size, leaving the customer to adjust them to fit a particular body. The pattern pieces are still the basic body and sleeve shapes. There are minimal, if any, instructions.

Simultaneously, a variety of dressmaking systems appeared, complete with pattern-making tools of various complexity and a series of calculations based upon an individual's measurements for full-scale women's and children's garments. These were marketed to professional dressmakers and home sewers. Excellent studies of these can be found in Claudia Kidwell's (1979) *Cutting a Fashionable Fit* and Patricia Trautman's (1987) *Clothing America*. Unlike the tailoring systems, these disappeared from the market by the early twentieth century.

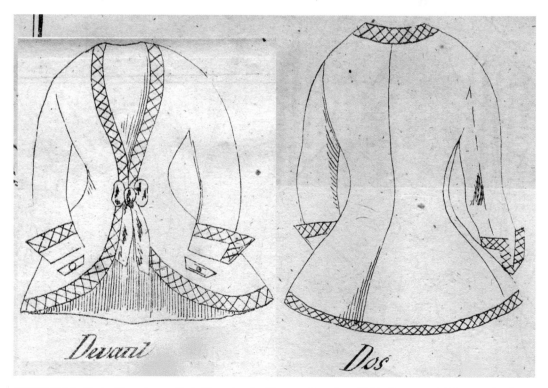

FIGURE 14 *Veste Circasienne*, Petit Courrier des Dames, *October 1847. Commercial Pattern Archive.*

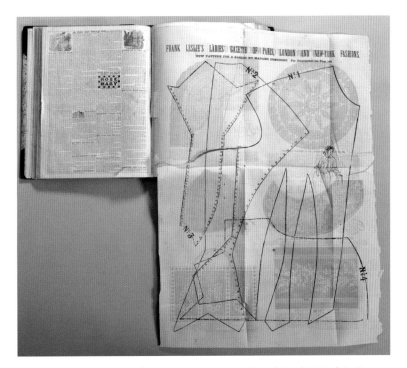

FIGURE 15 *Misses' Bodice, Demorest pattern*, Frank Leslie's Lady's Gazette of Fashion, *November 1854. Courtesy of the Kent State University Museum.*

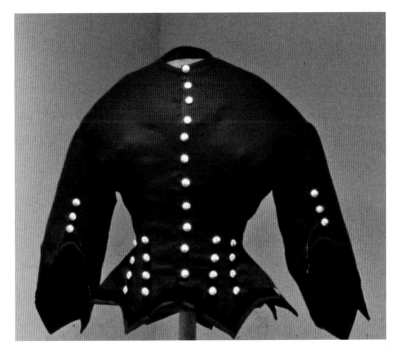

FIGURE 16 *Misses' Bodice, from 1854 Demorest pattern. Commercial Pattern Archive.*

Fashion Periodicals: 1850s

The editors of *The World of Fashion*, which had begun publication in 1824 in London, announced,

> We this month present to our subscribers and the public, in addition to the customary attractions of this favored magazine, the FIRST COLLECTION OF PATTERNS for Fashionable dresses and Millinery which we propose continuing every month in order that Ladies of Distinction and their milliners and dressmakers may possesses the utmost facilities for constructing their costumes with most approved taste and in highest and most perfect style of fashion. (*World of Fashion*, August 1850: n.p.)

These full-size patterns were in one size only with pattern sections superimposed on each other, as shown in Figure 15.

Another London publication, *Le Follet Journal du Grand Mode*, began publishing in 1846 and included dressmaker patterns with each issue (Seligman 1996: 217). By 1858, *The Englishwomen's Domestic Magazine*, published in London by the Beetons, was including full-size pattern sheets.

A popular American periodical, *Godey's Ladies Book*,[4] began publishing in 1830. In December 1851, *Godey's* announced the formation of a new department for ordering patterns beginning in

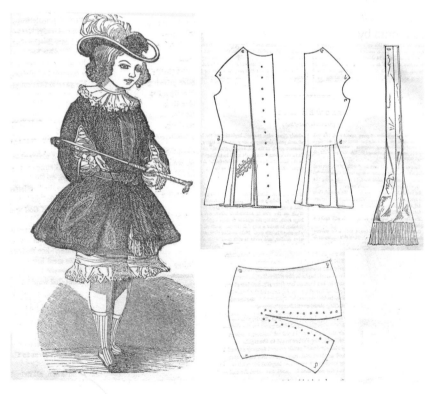

FIGURE 17 *Boys' Tunic Dress and Pattern Diagram,* Godey's Lady's Book, *April 1853. Commercial Pattern Archive.*

January 1852. The January issue of 1853 advertises "Cloak Patterns—or indeed any kind of pattern can now be purchased in this city [Philadelphia]." The cloak pattern cost about $1.25 (equivalent to $32.25 in 2011) and "will be procured by the editress of the fashion department, who has supplied such orders the past month" (91). That year *Godey's* began including pattern diagrams, proportional small-scale drawings of the pattern shape. In most instances, scale is not given. The Boys' Tunic Dress was the first (April 1853: 365) (see Figure 17).

Frank Leslie's Lady's Gazette of Fashion started in 1854 in New York, declaring,

> Our objective is to improve the standard of our own national fashions, to give encouragement to the great talent that exists everywhere among us, in all branches of industry, to impart, in this particular, nationality and dignity to those branches of the industrial arts so usefully exercised in designing and fabricating ladies' garments. . . . We are prepared to furnish paper patterns of the newest styles in any department of ladies' costume. (January 1854: 2)

The January issue contained an overlay pattern sheet for a basque waist and a French waist. There is no illustration, nor is the pattern identified. However, the February issue contains a Mme Demorest mantilla pattern, as does the September issue, with a drawing on the overlaid pattern sheet. These sheets were supplements tucked into each issue. Consequently, many have been lost. (The inclusion of free supplement pattern sheets was a practice copied by other publications to attract women subscribers.)

Peterson's Magazine started in 1842 and was carrying proportional diagrams of women's and children's garments by January 1857 (see Figure 18). It should be noted that the diagrams did not

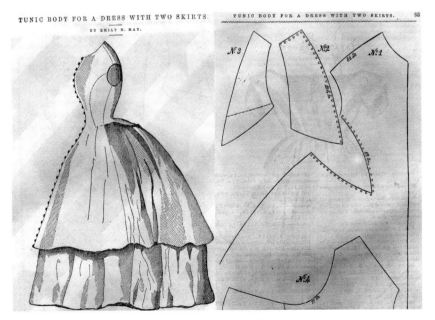

FIGURE 18 *Tunic Body for a Dress with Two Skirts Pattern Diagram*, Peterson's, *January 1857. Commercial Pattern Archive.*

indicate the scale, rarely gave measurements, and only offered the briefest of instruction for making up the garment. In contrast, *Arthur's Home Magazine* avowed that

> frankly, . . . our fashion department is the one in which we take the least interest. . . . We look to something higher and more enduring. . . . Still, . . . it [fashion] has the rule in magazines of this class . . . therefore [we] have completed an arrangement with Madame Demorest of New York to supply us monthly with such styles are in vogue . . . and yet not make fashion an imperious tyrant. (*Arthur's*, July 1866: 63)

Arthur's fashion department was dropped in 1872 only to be reinstated in 1873, and the patterns were to be ordered directly from Butterick.

The popularity of Paris fashions probably inspired S.T. Taylor of New York to import and publish a triumvirate of French fashion magazines in English. Beginning with *Dress-Maker and Milliner's Guide* in 1852, Taylor followed with *Le Bon Ton* in 1853 and *Le Petite Massager* in 1865 (see Figure 19). His aim was to promote French fashions and sell his dressmaking drafting system and full-size

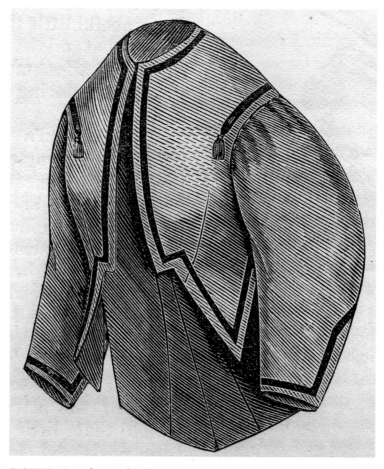

FIGURE 19 *Indoor Jacket,* Le Bon Ton, *1867. Commercial Pattern Archive.*

patterns plain or trimmed. Trimmed patterns had the body of the garment in one color paper with decorative details, such as braiding, in a different color to allow the purchaser to see the full effect of the garment. Both Taylor and Demorest use this method to better illustrate how the final garment should appear. To entice subscribers to his magazines, Taylor included pattern diagrams and a free full-size pattern in each issue by the late 1850s (see Figure 19).

Handbooks: 1840s–1850s

Noting the popularity of early instructional manuals and dressmaking tips in periodicals, publishers on both sides of the Atlantic introduced new how-to publications for the home sewer. Noteworthy English titles include *The Ladies Handbook of Millinery, Dressmaking and Tatting* (1843) and *The Art of Dressmaking, Containing Plain Directions in Simple Language from the Fitting of the Pattern to the Finish of the Dress* (1849). In America, nearly identical instructions are published in *The American Ladies' Memorial* (1850) and *The Ladies' Self Instructor* ([1853] 1988). In the latter, the anonymous author speaks of girls learning dressmaking very early by clothing their dolls and making paper patterns for their bodices. The dolls have a distinct advantage because they "lie very still to be fitted." The advice for cutting out a dress, whether for a doll or an adult, is to

> first measure off the number of breadths of the proper lengths for the skirt which is, of course to be regulated by the height of the wearer and the manner in which it is intended to be made and try them on one side. If tucks are to be introduced into the skirt, a proper allowance must be made for these, as do for the turnings both at the top and bottom. You next cut out the sleeves, as being the largest part of the garment, except for the skirt. In cutting out the sleeves you must first prepare a paper pattern of the required shape. (135)

The author gives no hints as to how to prepare the paper pattern. *The Art of Dressmaking* recommends the use of Holland, a lightweight, plain-weave linen, instead of paper, which would make preparing and fitting the pattern easier and have greater durability than paper. The author continues with instructions for making the pattern for a bodice:

> [P]roceed to take the proper measures of the front and back of the body, by fitting a paper pattern to the shape of the person for whom the dress is intended. The paper should be thin and you commence by folding down the corner the length of the front, and pinning it to the middle stay-bone. Then spread the paper as smoothly as possible along the bosom to the shoulder, and fold it in a plait, so as to fit the shape exactly, and bring the paper under the arm, making it retain its position by a pin; from this point you cut it off downward under the arm, and along the waist; the paper is then to be rounded for the arm-hole and the shoulder, and you must recollect to leave it large enough to admit of the turnings. (*Ladies' Self Instructor* [1853] 1988: 136)

The process is repeated for the back. It is little wonder why the published paper patterns were so popular, even though they only came in one size. A considerable amount of time and probably frustration was saved with the paper patterns.

Summary

By mid-century, publication of books of advice and instruction for the home sewer in the art of dressmaking flourished, and there was an abundance of women's periodicals with fashion news. Several of these were offering proportional scaled patterns or full-size patterns by individuals such as Mrs. Folett in England and Mme Demorest in America. Large pullout sheets with overlaid pattern pieces were becoming more prevalent. Both pattern formats were continued into the next decades, but the full-size pattern would ultimately supplant the small-scale patterns. However, full-size dress patterns came in only one size. The user had the problem of adjusting them to whatever body the garment was intended to fit. The patterns included only the minimum pattern pieces, such as body front and back and sleeves. There were no facings, plackets, pockets, and so forth, and in the case of women's garments, no skirts or ruffles. Inclusion of skirt patterns was generally considered unnecessary since the skirts were rectangular, requiring only an arrangement of pleats to fit to the waist measurement. Although vastly improved since the early part of the century, the patterns available in the early 1850s left much to be desired. The development of new technology and consumer services in the next decades paved the way for the emergence of the profitable pattern industry in the coming years.

3

Nineteenth-century Technology

The two earliest U.S. pattern companies devoted to creating patterns for dressmakers and home sewers were Demorest (1853–1854) and Butterick (1863–1864). The success of these companies was enabled by new technology. Prior to the 1850s, women relied on skilled dressmakers or on themselves for the latest fashionable outfits as well as for more utilitarian garments, such as housedresses, sleepwear, basic undergarments, and children's clothing.

For fashionable garments, those families who could afford to do so were advised in *Godey's Lady's Magazine*, "A dressmaker's charge is seventy-five cents a day, and, including mantillias and capes, no family can well dispense with less than a week's service every season." However, women were strongly encouraged to develop their own dressmaking skills. *Godey's* further admonished young ladies not to consider dressmaking "vulgar," for as the editors suggest, "You may consent to share the fortune of some noble minded adventurer in the new country—California or Minesota [*sic*]. . . . As an American woman in this era you may be placed in many positions quite as remote. And then what becomes of the helpless?" (September 1851: 192).

New technology opened a variety of opportunities for expanding fashion-related enterprises by the mid-nineteenth century. The most notable was the sewing machine and its manufacture. The invention of flexible, portable dress forms simplified home production of clothing. In addition, John Tebbel in *The Magazine in America 1741–1900* observed that fashion-related publications increased like a "veritable tsunami between 1825 and 1850 induced by the technological breakthrough in printing with the inventions of the cylinder press, and the rapid growth of a highly literate population" (Tebbel and Zuckerman 1991: 8). Moreover, steam-driven paper-making machines produced paper from wood pulp, which was much less expensive than rag or cloth pulp paper. All these ingredients enabled the expansion of the tissue paper pattern industry.

The Sewing Machine

Inventors were experimenting with mechanical sewing by the mid-eighteenth century, but it was not until the mid-nineteenth century that a functioning, practical machine was invented by Barthélemy Thimonnier. In "A Brief History of the Sewing Machine," Graham Forsdyke explains that

Thimonnier's machine was granted a French patent in 1830. By 1840, he had installed eighty of his machines in his factory for sewing uniforms for the French army. Parisian tailors, who feared the machine would put craftsmen tailors out of work, destroyed his machines, and Thimonnier was forced to flee to England. The fear of mechanized sewing persisted throughout a large part of the nineteenth century.[1]

Elias Howe claimed the invention of the first practical sewing machine and received a patent in 1846. The needle action on Howe's machine was side to side and it was powered with a hand crank. Isaac Singer perfected a simplified machine in 1851. The needle action on Singer's machine was up and down, rather than side to side and it was powered with a foot pedal, which made it more efficient than Howe's. However, Isaac Singer's machine used the same double, looped thread lockstitch that Howe had patented, which led to a long series of lawsuits. Meanwhile, other sewing machine manufacturers, including Wheeler & Wilson (1854–1855) and Grover, Baker & Co. (1851), were also busy manufacturing machines. At the conclusion of the lawsuits and to combat the rising competition, Singer, Howe, Wheeler & Wilson, and Grover, Baker & Co. pooled their patents, which required all other manufacturers to obtain a license to make their machines and pay $15 (equivalent to $406 in 2011) per machine until 1877, when the last patent expired, allowing prices for machines to drop (see Figures 20, 21, and 22).

The original models were heavy and intended for the manufacture of ready-to-wear clothing. Kidwell and Christman's (1974) comprehensive study on the development of ready-made clothing noted that the ready-made clothing industry benefited greatly from the invention of the sewing machine because the garments could be made more quickly with a machine than by hand. Even tailors began producing "ready-made" garments to fill in work between the winter and summer seasons for their bespoke trade, but not necessarily with the aid of the sewing machine, which was regarded as only capable of producing substandard results (46–47).

FIGURE 20 *Grover, Baker & Co. Sewing Machine Ad.* Scott's Mirror of Fashion, *June 16, 1854. Commercial Pattern Archive.*

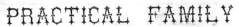

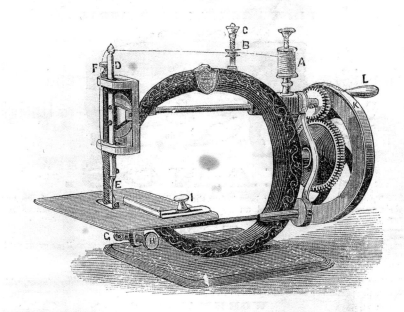

FIGURE 21 *Bartlett's Sewing Machine.* Demorest's Monthly Magazine, *May 1866. Commercial Pattern Archive.*

By 1856, a lightweight machine was designed for use in the home. It cost $125 (equivalent to $2,997 in 2010) at a time when the average yearly income was $500 (equivalent to $11,985 in 2010). *Godey's Lady's Book* suggested that ten families in each country village should pool their money and buy one machine. Singer's partner, Edward Clark, devised the hire-purchase system, which offered women the opportunity to rent a machine and apply the rental to the purchase price—$5 down and the rest to be paid with interest. About a decade later, Butterick Pattern Co. advised new brides with $1.00 to invest $0.50 in a Bible and $0.50 toward a good sewing machine. There is further advice addressed to

[y]oung men and ladies who are just sipping the sweets of connubial felicity, before you get a bedstead, purchase a sewing machine. If you can't have both, sleep on the floor until you can earn

FIGURE 22 *Sewing Machine Advertisement after Singer's Patent Expired.* Demorest's Monthly Magazine, *January 1889. Commercial Pattern Archive.*

enough with your sewing machine to pay for a bed-stead. Saw off halve a dozen pieces of maple boards for dinner plates, . . . [use] logs for seats. (*Butterick Catalog* ca. 1869: n.p.) (see Figure 23)

In general, tailors were slow to take on the idea of machine sewing, especially for their custom trade. In 1853, *Minister's Gazette of Fashion* cautions, "[A]s a substitute for sewing by hand, in its present powers, the idea cannot be for one moment entertained. It performs but one description of stitch—the back stitch; and it will therefore, not require too much argument to our readers the impossibility of a garment being completed solely by means of the machine" (23). As late as the 1890s, arguments were still raging in the tailoring journals over whether good tailoring could be done by machine.

Women, on the other hand, took to the sewing machine immediately. Women's periodicals, such as *Godey's*, published articles encouraging the use of the machine. They announced that the sewing machine was "capable of sewing every part of a garment, except for buttons and button holes. . . . It is so *simple* in its construction and action that it may be worked by a *child*, and will sew in a circle, curve, or turn a square corner, equally well as a straight line" (February 1854: 127). There is no mention of a manufacturer, but an almost identical announcement from the Lancashire (England) Company's patentee, Mr. C.T. Judikins, appeared in the September 1853 issue of the *Minister's Gazette of Fashion*. The announcement must have been paid for since the editors countered with their caution to tailors in the September editorial (23). Clearly, there was ambiguity over the advantages and disadvantages of mechanized sewing.

SEWING MACHINE COSTUME.

FIGURE 23 *Sewing Machine Costume.* Butterick Catalog, *inside cover, ca. 1869, with a Wheeler & Wilson sewing machine. Commercial Pattern Archive.*

While there was a great deal of concern over the potential loss of jobs for tailors, there was also concern about the effect the sewing machine would have on women. Williams commented that "many men wanted to believe that women couldn't handle such a complicated piece of machinery; they feared that if women did perform their sewing duties in less time there would be time left over for them to improve themselves or participate in the suffrage movement" (Williams Papers: Early History Notes). That fear was countered in many publications including *Frank Leslie's Lady's Gazette of Fashions*: "Women are not yet wholly superseded, being extremely useful in their appropriate place—in fact, absolutely indispensable; yet the improvement attempted by the sewing machine has exerted an important influence on her social state." The article concludes that the "sewing machine promises permanent relief to wearisome bondage to the needle-woman" (September 1856: 120).

With the widespread availability (and acceptance) of this new mechanical marvel, the profes-sional seamstress could earn appreciably more money than sewing by hand. The individual home sewer trying to clothe herself and her family could also produce a vastly increased number of gar-ments. The only thing holding them back was the lack of reliable patterns and the means for getting the patterns to those who did not live in urban communities with establishments offering them.

U.S. Postal Service

Changes in the U.S. Postal Service provided a solution for distributing patterns. In 1845, the ser-vice, heretofore limited to personal letters, expanded to accept lithograph circulars, handbills, and all other printed material. The expanded service allowed fashion-related publications to be sent to even the most remote location. The service also introduced post office money orders for send-ing money securely by mail. (The Royal Post Office in Britain introduced a money order system in 1838.) Moreover, the speed and efficiency of the mail service was improved by the wide network of new railroads across the United States. The expanded service permitted selling subscriptions for periodicals and other items, such as patterns, and delivering them by mail, thus creating a fer-tile environment for the newly developed mail-order businesses.

Dress Forms

A common problem for the home sewer and professional dressmaker was fitting a garment when it was being put together. Ideally, one wanted a dress form, or dummy, with the appropri-ate measurements of the future wearer. In general, the forms were for the torso only, usually made of papier-mâché with a thin layer of padding and covered with fabric. But the fashion shift from simple pleated or gathered skirts to shaped skirts over hoops and then bustles in the latter decades of the nineteenth century required some support to achieve the best results. Further, corsets molded the female torso, altering proportions of bust to waist, depending on the preva-lent fashion. A clever solution to meet these needs was devised by Hall's Bazar Form Company. The shape of the torso was created using narrow bands of steel riveted together to make the figure, which could be expanded or compressed to required measurements. It could then be covered with fabric. The form for the skirt appears to have been inspired by umbrella ribs. It could be raised or lowered and collapsed for storage. An undated *Hall's Bazar Dress & Skirt Form* brochure announced that the skirt form was "adjustable to any height, from the shortest to the tallest, and any size, from the slightest figure to a 36-inch waist and 60-inch hip measure, and expands in a regular manner to throw out the skirt for train." One model offered a complete port-able form with the torso and skirt section designed to be combined or used separately. Another model featured a skirt form with support for a bustle folded into a box short enough to go into the shortest trunk for ladies who traveled and needed to hang out and support trunk-crushed skirts. The brochure includes reprints of several testimonials from fashion publishers including Mme Demorest: "Every lady who makes her own and children's dresses should have one of Hall's Bazar Portable Forms" (see Figures 24 and 25).

Scenes from Life,

"Oh, mercy me, boo-hoo,hoo. I've tried everyway imaginable to drape my dresses, and they never look presentable." No wonder she cried - she had never heard of Hall's Bazar Form.

FIGURE 24 Hall's Bazar Dress and Skirt Forms *Brochure, ca. 1889. Commercial Pattern Archive.*

Saving Time

Lengthens Life.

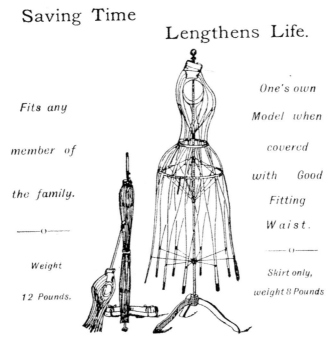

Fits any member of the family.

———o———

Weight 12 Pounds.

One's own Model when covered with Good Fitting Waist.

———o———

Skirt only, weight 8 Pounds

FIGURE 25 *Collapsible, Portable, Full-Figure Form in Two Parts, Torso and Skirt. "[F]olds like an umbrella."* Hall's Bazar Dress and Skirt Forms. *Commercial Pattern Archive.*

Summary

An improved U.S. Postal Service permitting mailing of a wide variety of materials including fashion periodicals, the availability of cheaper paper, and adjustable dress forms accelerated opportunities for home sewers to keep up with the latest fashions. More importantly, the sewing machine allowed a shorter time for making garments and stimulated greater complexity in the shape of women's fashions.

By the end of the 1860s, the cut of women's garments changed radically. Bodices changed from simple rectangular pieces with fitting darts to more complex, curving pieces seamed together to conform to the shape of the upper body. Skirts changed from simple rectangles gathered or pleated to fit the waist to more shaping with the use of gores (triangular pieces) seamed together to create new shapes, including bustles. Furthermore, skirts became more embellished with swags of material often draped in the back over a bustle structure. The changes required more seams, which could be sewn together efficiently on the sewing machine. The pace of fashion was accelerated through the fashion periodicals, the faster dissemination of materials, and the availability of patterns to create the latest styles (see Figures 26, 27, 28, 29, and 30).

TARTAN DRESS.

FIGURE 26 *Tartan Dress.* Demorest's Monthly Magazine, *December 1866. Commercial Pattern Archive.*

FIGURE 27 *Woman in 1860s Blue Dress. Perrin Collection, 1964.15.34. Courtesy of the University of Rhode Island Historic Textile and Costume Collection.*

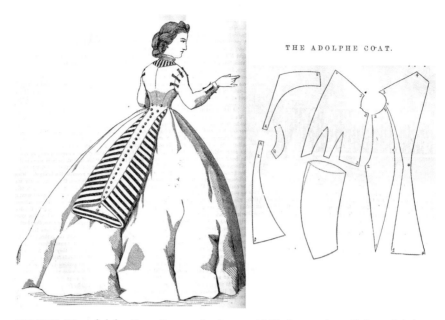

FIGURE 28 *Adolphe Coat.* Peterson's, *August 1864. Seven pieces (left to right): reverse for basque of tails behind, collar, front, sleeve upper and lower, side piece, and back. Commercial Pattern Archive.*

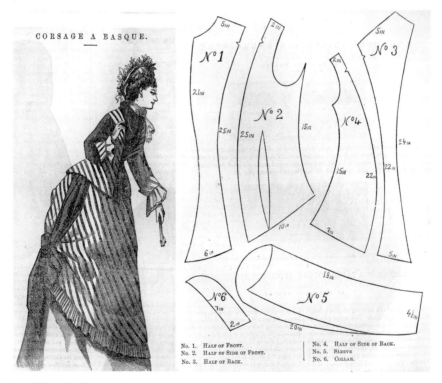

FIGURE 29 *Corsage Basque.* Peterson's, *July 1876. Commercial Pattern Archive.*

FIGURE 30 *House or Street Toilette. Demorest patterns: skirt, overdress with waist, plain and round back with pointed basques; $0.30 each.* Demorest's Monthly Magazine, *October 1872. Commercial Pattern Archive.*

4

Early History of Pattern Companies
1860s–1880s

The Companies

Demorest, the first to mass-produce retail patterns for the home sewer in the United States, took advantage of the expanded postal services selling by mail order as well as in retail outlets. Who the actual designer of the first patterns was is somewhat unclear. Mrs. Margaret Demorest (née Poole) is listed as Mme Demorest in *Leslie's Lady's Gazette of Fashion* in July 1854. However, it is believed that William Jennings Demorest employed Ellen Louise Curtis and her sister Kate from the early 1850s to create the patterns. Ellen is generally credited with the pattern designs. A year after Margaret's death, Ellen and William Jennings Demorest were married and Ellen became the acknowledged Mme Demorest.

Demorest patterns were available plain or trimmed. Patterns were made with colored paper with contrasting paper for trims. When the pattern was pinned together, it was ideal for display and promoting sales. Demorest advertised patterns in *Godey's Lady's Book* and, in 1854, included full-size patterns as supplements in *Leslie's Gazette of Fashion*. (See Figures 15 and 16.) The enterprise was so successful that in the late 1850s the company moved from Philadelphia to New York and began publishing *Mme Demorest's Quarterly & Mirror of Fashion* in 1860. It was the first in a number of publications, quarterly and monthly, with variations of the title. *Demorest's Monthly Magazine* was published until 1899 (Mott 1938: vol. 3, 325). The first issue lists four branches of Mme Demorest's showrooms, *magasins des modes*, as far west as Wisconsin and Missouri. By 1865 over 150 branches are listed, including in Canada.

Free Demorest patterns included as supplements in periodicals were for separate garments on over-printed sheets. They also sold tissue paper patterns for bodices, basques, sleeves, skirts, overskirts, children's clothing, and similar garments for $0.25 or made up and elegantly trimmed for $0.50. Complete sets for a garment were available to professional dressmakers for reduced rates. Patterns were available by mail order, at select retail shops, at dressmaker's establishments, or at Mme Demorest's Pattern Emporium in New York (Emery 1999: 237). Another option was for the individual to send measurements to Mme Demorest to have a special pattern made.

Demorest began offering patterns in sizes in 1871. The November issue of *Demorest's Monthly Magazine* announced the patterns were "each put in a neat envelope with a large illustration for the enclosed pattern printed on the face, full instructions for putting it together, and valuable suggestions in reference to material, trimming and quantity required" (November 1871: 343). Prices ranged from $0.15 for children's clothes to $0.60 (equivalent to $10.64 in 2011) for some ladies' costumes. Demorest patterns are identified with a name rather than a number.

S.T. Taylor, publisher of the English version of *Le Bon Ton*, was producing full-scale tissue patterns inspired by French fashions, which he included in each issue of the monthly publication by 1861. The patterns were in one size only and were intended for milliners and dressmakers (Penny [1863] 1996: 330). Taylor also had a dressmaking system—"Taylor's Dress Cutting Simplified and Reduced to Science"—so he was familiar with pattern grading or scaling a pattern to a different size by increments at important points using an algorithm in the clothing (Trautman 1987: 3) (see Figure 31).

760
Imp. Mariton.

LE BON TON

FIGURE 31 *French Fashions.* Bon Ton, *January 1867. Commercial Pattern Archive.*

FIGURE 32 *Boys' Single-breasted Garibaldi Jacket 488 and Boys' Pants 1894.* Butterick Catalogue, *Fall 1871. Commercial Pattern Archive.*

Ebenezer Butterick entered the market in 1863–1864. A not too successful tailor, Butterick began offering boys' shirts, trousers, jackets, and a Garibaldi suit for boys (see Figure 32), reputedly his most popular pattern. Patterns were in sizes based upon the child's age. Furthermore, he took out a patent on his patterns, something that Demorest did not do, although Demorest did patent many other products.

In her unpublished "History of Butterick Pattern Company," Dorothy Rockwell writes that Butterick was so encouraged by his successful enterprise that he moved from Massachusetts to New York by the spring of 1864 (Rockwell ca. 1964: 4). His first publication, following Read's example (discussed in chapter 1), is a print of *Juvenile Fashions* by Currier (before his partnership with Ives) circa 1864. The print is inscribed, "This is my first printing. E. Butterick." He published the *Semi-Annual Report of Gent's Fashions* in 1865. Butterick's prices were competitive: vest patterns were $0.25 and frock coat patterns were $0.50; a dealer could purchase a set of fifty patterns for $5.00 (equivalent to $69.00 in 2011).

By 1866, Butterick had expanded his business to include sized patterns for girls and women, which quickly became a major part of his business. He published the *Ladies' Quarterly Report of Broadway Fashions* in the spring of 1867, which he expanded to *Metropolitan*, a monthly magazine devoted to selling women's patterns, in 1868. Most of the women's patterns were for separate sections of garments, such as bodices and skirts, and available in ten sizes based on bust measurements of twenty-eight to forty-six inches. The *Metropolitan* reported that Butterick was selling in excess of 1,500 patterns a day in 1871; however, that is most likely company hyperbole (Williams Papers). A review of their catalogs in 1871 indicates that they produced 450 new pattern styles during that year in various sizes (see Figures 33 and 34).

One of the most influential magazines to offer one-size-only patterns was *Harper's Bazar*, introduced in November 1867, based on *Der Bazar*. (The term "bazar" refers generally to a marketplace and was used freely by the nineteenth-century pattern companies to refer to their stock of patterns.) The title changed to *Harper's Bazaar* in 1929. From the outset, the weekly publication

FIGURE 33 *Ladies' Costumes. Patterns for the skirts and jackets sold separately at $0.20 to $0.30 each.* Butterick Metropolitan, *August 1872. Skirt 2207 $0.30; jacket 2308 $0.20; skirt back view "unornamented, which is a consideration, because it has to pass through the ordeal of washing & ironing." Commercial Pattern Archive.*

FIGURE 34 *Misses' Costumes. Patterns for skirts, overskirts, jackets, and waist sold separately, price $0.15 to $0.30.* Butterick Metropolitan, *August 1872. Commercial Pattern Archive.*

included overlaid pattern sheets as supplements in each issue. The sheets are printed on both sides and often contained twenty-five or more patterns. The patterns are for the basic shape of a garment and one size only; the size is often not given on the early sheets. The sheets could also contain embroidery patterns as well as patterns for various household items such as lampshades and fly swatters. A weekly publication, it issued fifty-two pattern sheets each year (see Figures 35 and 36).

The pattern pieces are superimposed and are defined by different types of lines (e.g. solid, broken, dashes and stars, dashes and darts, etc.). The shapes must be traced on separate transparent paper to obtain the piece and preserve the sheet. Overlay pattern sheets were included until 1913, when they were phased out. At the same time, noting the success of Demorest's and Butterick's individual patterns, Harper's added individual cut paper patterns to their product line in 1870.

The success of the Demorest and Butterick patterns inspired other would-be entrepreneurs to try the pattern business. One of the most successful was James McCall. Originally trained as a tailor in Glasgow, Scotland, McCall immigrated to New York in 1869 and worked as a tailor and agent for the "Royal Chart" drafting system and as an agent for Wheeler & Wilson's Elliptic Sewing Machines (Walsh 1979: 304). McCall published the *Catalog of the Bazar Paper Patterns*; the name for his patterns was no accident (see Figure 37). He was consciously affiliating himself, without any legal connection, to *Harper's Bazar*. McCall's 1871 fall catalog announces,

FIGURE 35 Harper's Bazar, *November 1867. Commercial Pattern Archive.*

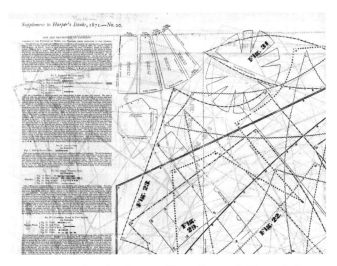

FIGURE 36 *Overlay Pattern Sheet (Portion).* Harper's Bazar, *1871. Commercial Pattern Archive.*

FIGURE 37 *Regina Jacket and Overdress 270; Alberta Polinaise with Cape and Sacque 269; Adelina Polonaise 219; Lady's Sacque and Overdress with Sash 134.* Catalogue of the Bazar Paper Patterns *published by James McCall, Fall 1871. Commercial Pattern Archive.*

Every pattern we issue will be the product of the ablest and most experienced gentleman-dressmaker in the country; all under the supervision of Mr H Moschowitz, a gentleman who stands at the head of his profession, and who is unquestionably the ablest and most experienced dressmaker in the United States. What Worth is to Paris, Moschowitz is to New York. (*Catalog of the Bazar Paper Patterns* 1871: n.p.)

Following the established practice of capitalizing on identifiable name recognition, McCall published *The Queen; Illustrating McCall's Bazar Glove-Fitting Patterns*, a fashion periodical, in 1873. It was devoted to woodcut prints of the garments for each pattern offered with some brief notes on the latest modes (Mott 1938: vol. 4, 580). McCall was obviously trying to associate his patterns with the high fashion and society depicted in the British society publication *The Queen*. The periodical was renamed *The Queen of Fashion* in 1891 and then *McCall's* in 1897.

Pattern production was lucrative enough that a number of new pattern companies were formed during the early 1870s. Mr. Annesley Burdette Smith, a New York real estate broker, developed a different approach to promoting his patterns. Instead of tissue paper models or illustrations with a pattern, he provided "cloth models." Approximately one-eighth scale, the pattern pieces are half of the garment piece—as in half of the front bodice and half of the back bodice—to be cut on the fold. The model is hand-sewn and packaged with the tissue pattern. Information on the pattern was stamped on one of the tissue pieces. His patterns were one size only. Smith actively promoted his patterns with advertisements in various magazines as well as his own catalog, *Smith's Illustrated Pattern Bazar* and *Elite Dressmaker and Milliner* (see Figures 38 and 39).

FIGURE 38 *Cloth Pattern. A. B. Smith, ca. 1873. Commercial Pattern Archive.*

FIGURE 39 *Misses' Gown. A. B. Smith*, Smith's Illustrated Pattern Bazar, *ca. 1873. Commercial Pattern Archive.*

Domestic Sewing Machine Company expanded to include patterns in the early 1870s and introduced *Domestic Monthly*, an illustrated magazine of fashion and literature, in 1873. It contained a catalog of the latest patterns with sizes and prices. Sizes ranged from a thirty- to forty-six-inch bust for women and a thirty-two- to forty-eight-inch chest for men and a range of ages one to fifteen years for children; the price range was generally $0.15–0.30. The editors included regular dressmaking columns, color plates, and, of course, promotions for the Domestic Sewing Machine (see Figure 40).

Other new pattern companies selling patterns through mail order or from agents in the 1870s included Ehrlich & Company, Andrew's Bazar, the Ladies' Bazar, and New York & Paris Fashion Co. Only Ehrlich lasted until 1889.

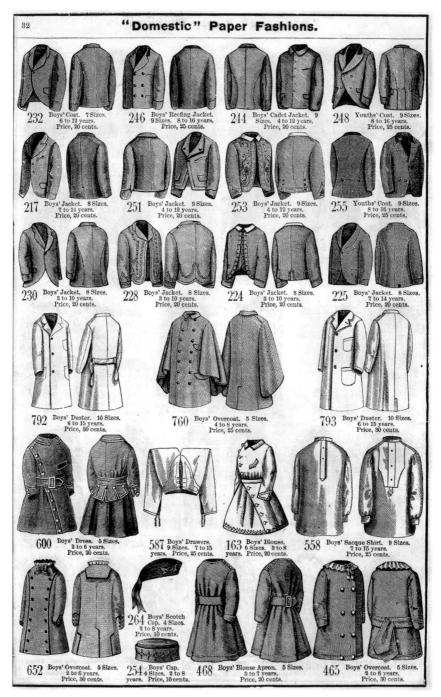

FIGURE 40 *Boys' Patterns*. Catalogue of the Domestic Paper Fashions, *Spring–Summer 1875*. *Commercial Pattern Archive.*

English and French Pattern Companies

Outside the United States, already established publications such as Beetons' *The Englishwomen's Domestic Magazine* began selling patterns by Mme Goubaud in 1860 (Adburgham 1989: 110). Mme Schild offered patterns starting in 1868 and published several periodicals. In 1878, *The London and Paris Ladies' Magazine of Fashion* announced it was offering Devere "Paris Model Patterns" and began including a full-size tissue paper pattern sheet with each issue in 1879. R. S. Cartwright published several fashion-related publications including the *Practical Family Dressmaker*, offering Leach's pattern supplement sheets and mail-order patterns beginning in 1878. The following year a former employee of the Beetons', Christopher Weldon, started his own enterprise offering mail-order patterns and pattern supplement sheets. Weldon's enterprise published fifty fashion-related magazines with various titles between 1879 and 1950 (Seligman 2003: 97–101).

French publications included *Le Toilette de Paris*, begun in 1858 with full-size patterns in each issue, and *Journal des Demoiselles* (combined with *Petite Currier des Dames* by 1840), offering full-size pattern sheets and embroidery patterns (see Figure 41).

FIGURE 41 *Corsage à Basque. Pattern sheet,* Journal des Demoiselles et Petit Courrier des Dames Renis, *October 1870. Commercial Pattern Archive.*

Tissue Paper Pattern Production

Few early Demorest, Tailor, or Butterick patterns have survived. Other than supplements, the only examples of early practices are Butterick patterns. The pattern has the folded pieces secured by a single pin with a printed label identifying the garment, the size, and a brief description of the pattern pieces glued to the package. There is no illustration or any facing pieces. The instructions are minimal at best (see Figure 42). The label attached to a Butterick boys' sack coat circa 1864 states,

> This pattern consists of a BACK, FRONT, UPPER AND UNDER SLEEVE, COLLAR, AND POCKET BANDS (pattern label capitols). The Sleeve is to be sewed with the longest seam to be placed at the notch on the back and the hollowing side of the sleeve is to be sewed into the lowest part of the arm-scye [under the arm]. The Pocket Bands to be bound with binding, the garment is to be bound. Bindings are fashionable. Age: 9 Years; quantity of cloth—2 Yards. (Commercial Pattern Archive)

The pattern pieces are cut from tissue and notched to provide matching points. Demorest began packaging patterns in envelopes by 1871. Butterick did adopt their use later, but sporadically.

Tissue pattern production practices established in the 1860s became commonplace by the 1870s. Full-size pattern pieces were cut from lightweight paper. Each piece has notches on the edge to show where that piece joined the next. A series of holes, triangles, and squares were punched in each piece to indicate darts, pleats, and other internal requirements for shaping

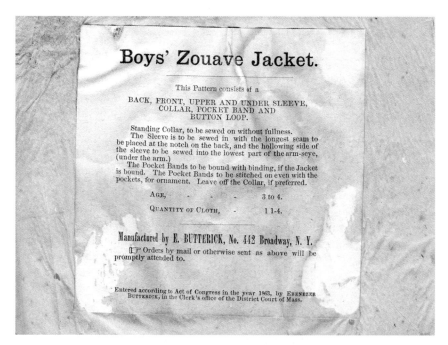

FIGURE 42 *Boys' Zouave Jacket. Butterick Pattern Label, ca. 1864. Commercial Pattern Archive.*

the flat piece to the rounded shape of the body. Dubbed "cut and punched," this was the only type of tissue pattern available until the 1920s. Cut and punched patterns continued into the 1990s because production costs were considerably lower than those requiring the setup of machinery for printing a small run of patterns (see Figure 43).[1]

The process begins with the sketch of the garment, typically by an in-house artist, and then an expert dressmaker makes a cloth model. After testing for accuracy of fit, the model is taken apart and used to make the master pattern. The master is placed on stacks of tissue paper and held in place by large, round metal weights. The master is traced on the top sheet of tissue along with all internal markings. The sheets are cut by hand with a special knife, and notches are cut

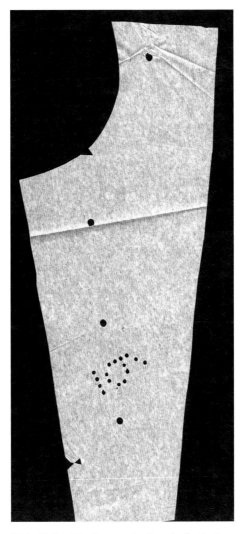

FIGURE 43 *Cut and Punched Facing. Standard Designer 8424, 1925. Commercial Pattern Archive.*

into the edge of the piece. Codes of internal holes to indicate grain lines, piece numbers, darts, and so forth were rendered with steel punches and a mallet. Pattern pieces, such as the sleeve, were usually identified with a letter made of holes punched through the tissue. The cut pieces for each garment were assembled and folded by hand. The package was identified with the pattern company name, style number, drawing of the design, and whatever instructions were given. If this information was on a label, it was glued to the pattern package or put in the appropriate envelope (see Figures 44 and 45).

Making patterns expanded employment opportunities for women. No longer confined to the role of needlewoman "shirtmaker," women were hired to make and sell patterns. Penny's survey of employment for women between October 1859 and November 1861 in New York City found that both Demorest and Taylor employed women to design, make cloth models and masters, cut patterns, fold, package, and sell the patterns (Penny [1863] 1996: 330). Ross states the Demorests employed over 200 women at the end of the Civil War (Ross 1963: 24).

Marketing Patterns

Pattern companies promoted pattern sales in women's magazines and pattern catalogs distributed to sales outlets. The women's magazines tended to fall into two categories: those that addressed a broad range of women's interests and those devoted to fashions and the sale of patterns. McCall's *Queen of Fashion*, for example, contained nothing except illustrations and descriptions of McCall patterns. Butterick added the *Delineator* in 1873 to their publications. Although the main objective was to sell Butterick patterns, it also contained articles on dressmaking techniques and millinery and other editorial content. *Domestic Monthly* took a similar approach but added literature to its content. Magazines with a broader focus included *Godey's*, *Peterson's*, *Frank Leslie's Lady's Gazette*, and *Englishwomen's Domestic Magazine*. These periodicals, however, continued to include proportional pattern drafts and/or full-scale pattern supplements into the 1880s.

Demorest periodicals bridged both categories. In 1865, Demorest renamed the magazine *Demorest's Illustrated Monthly* and incorporated *Mme Demorest's Mirror of Fashion* in the magazine, thus allowing Demorest to promote his social causes though a series of articles. For example, they were ardent abolitionists and hired several African American women who were integrated in the workrooms and company social gatherings.

At the same time, the pattern companies began issuing separate catalogs containing a large assortment of patterns. The catalogs ranged in sizes. For example, Butterick's 1879 *The Metropolitan* was large, 17 by 15.5 inches with approximately 250 pages, and is the forerunner of today's counter catalog. Others were small quarto-size booklets of twenty-five to thirty pages, usually issued quarterly. The latter usually had space for the name of a fabric store to be printed on the catalog. This practice continued well into the twentieth century.

Sizing

Perhaps more crucial to success for pattern sales was the practice of making patterns available in a range of sizes. The first to offer sized patterns was Butterick; as a former tailor, he applied

FIGURE 44 *Stacked Pattern Tissue Sheets for Cutting.* McCall Spring Quarterly, *1924. Commercial Pattern Archive.*

FIGURE 45 *Folding Patterns.* Modern Miss, *Winter 1951. Commercial Pattern Archive.*

the proportional approach. For children, he used age to determine the proportions, designating patterns for three to six years or nine years, for example. For adults, the proportions system was based on the bust or chest measure for bodices and dresses and waist measurement for skirts combined with height. Generally, the idealized height for women was five feet, five inches. The same proportional system was used by those who originally offered patterns in one size only, such as Demorest and Harper's. The size was usually for a five-foot, five-inch woman with a thirty-six-inch bust.

Current fashions and undergarments influenced proportional systems. As explained in Butterick's 1871 *The Metropolitan*, a lady with a bust measure of thirty-two inches usually has a twenty-four-inch waist, or eight inches less than the bust, but a miss of ten years usually has a bust measure of twenty-seven inches with the waist usually twenty-four inches. By 1905, when the flat-front corset was in vogue, the proportion for the thirty-two-inch bust changed to a twenty-two-inch waist. Using age for children and young women, the age became the designation for size. For example, size twelve was the size of an average twelve-year-old with a bust measure of twenty-nine inches and waist twenty-one inches.

Summary

Tissue paper patterns for women's and children's clothes were intended for, and bought by, the home sewer. Off-the-rack clothing at modest prices was becoming readily available, but the bulk of women's and children's clothing was still made at home. Kidwell notes in *Cutting a Fashionable Fit* that women's close-fitting fashion in the last part of the nineteenth century did not lend itself to the proportional sizing necessary for mass production of ready-to-wear and was the major reason that such a high proportion of women's wear continued to be made by the home sewer or dressmaker (Kidwell 1979: 20).

By the end of the 1870s, the foundation for the pattern industry was well established. Tissue paper pattern production practices had been refined to allow mass production. Publication of periodicals and catalogs became central to successful promotional and advertising policies. Packaging the patterns gradually improved to include illustrations of the garment, and in some instances, the pattern pieces were placed in envelopes rather than pinned together. The enterprises thrived and by the end of the decade were poised for expansion.

5

New Markets and Expansion

1880s–1900

U.S. Companies

By 1880, the six major U.S. pattern companies—Demorest, Butterick, McCall, Harper's Bazar, Taylor, and Domestic—had positioned themselves in the market. Each published a magazine advertising their patterns for the latest fashions for women, a full complement of children's clothing, undergarments for all, and shirts, trousers, and various other men's non-tailored garments.

Demorest's market was primarily aimed at the upper class, encouraging established dressmakers and milliners to buy packages of patterns and display cards featuring the designs and promoting the latest fashions. Another promotional scheme was the offer of designs featured only in *Demorest's Monthly Magazine* as premiums to subscribers. Patterns for designs like the 1888 Loretta basque, gored foundation skirt, and Loretta drapery were not for sale (see Figure 46). Each item required a coupon, which was only good for one month. The patterns were "not regular stock patterns" but "new and elegant designs upon which special care has been expended . . . gotten up new each month, exclusively for this Magazine, and can *only* be obtained through coupon orders contained in each monthly issue" (*Demorest's Monthly Magazine*, June 1888: 544). Non-coupon patterns could be purchased from national and international retail outlets and from Mme Demorest's Emporium. International sales are emphasized in the 1877 pattern catalog, in English, French, and German. The exchange rate for English prices was "one penny for two cents U.S. money" (Demorest 1877: 5).

From the outset, the patterns were for individual sections of a garment (e.g., bodices, sleeves, jackets, and the like) rather than whole outfits. The approach encouraged individually designed garments—a nineteenth-century mix and match. The practice was continued until the magazine ceased publication in 1899.

Butterick used the "Delineator" to promote a connection with the middle-class consumer with emphasis on children's and women's clothing for complete bodices, jackets, and skirts, which usually sold for slightly less than Demorest's individual pieces. Full women's costumes were added to the catalogs by 1873 for $0.50 to $0.75 ($0.50 equal to $8.99 in 2011). The patterns were offered in a range of sizes (see Figures 47 and 48).

McCall sought to bridge the gap. Their sized patterns for complete garments were aimed at the sophisticated client through advertising in their publications such as *The Queen* and through the use of cachet terms like "Bazar" and "Glove Fitting" (see Figure 49).

FIGURE 46 *Ladies' Costume. Loretta basque, gored foundation skirt, Loretta drapery, Demorest's Monthly Magazine, June 1888: 522. Commercial Pattern Archive. "[D]rapery finished with rows of machine stitching." Bust sizes thirty-four to forty inches; drapery medium size; skirt three sizes, waist twenty-three, twenty-five, and twenty-seven. Available only by coupon.*

FIGURE 47 *Ladies' Cycling Toilet. Jacket 9023, 1s3d or $0.30; shirtwaist 9021, 1s or $0.25; cycling skirt 1287, 1s or $0.25; leggings 1286, 7d or $0.15; hat, 5d or $0.10. Total cost 4s5d or $1.05.* Delineator, *May 1897. Commercial Pattern Archive.*

FIGURE 48 *Maternity Gown. Consisting of a blouse with fitted lining and a five-gore skirt 9183.* Delineator, *July 1897. Commercial Pattern Archive. The two back gores gathered and tacked to an elastic stay and casing for tapes in front and side gores; blouse lining close with front lacing cords; seven sizes thirty to forty-two inches, 1s6d or $0.35; twelve yards, twenty-eight inches wide.*

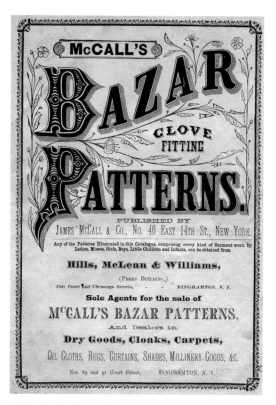

FIGURE 49 McCall's Bazar Glove Fitting Patterns Catalog, *1887. Commercial Pattern Archive.*

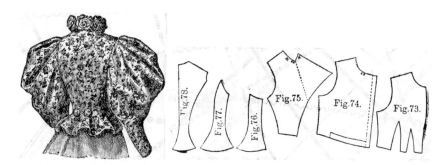

FIGURE 50 *Chiné Velvet Bodice with Diagram. Harper's Bazar Overlay Pattern Sheet 3, Figure X, September 15, 1895.7.BWS. Commercial Pattern Archive. Bodice back, sides, vest, front, and lining front. Sleeve pattern pieces not included in diagram.*

Harper's Bazar patterns were intended for the skilled sewer since the patterns were overlaid on large sheets and consisted of separate pieces for fitted garments. Skirts were either not included or shown as diagrams for the seamstress to draft to the necessary size. In some instances, diagrams of bodices and sleeves were included on the sheets (see Figure 50).

FIGURE 51 *Ladies' Princess Dress. Domestic 4934, 1891.29.URI. Commercial Pattern Archive.*

Taylor can be considered an active but peripheral pattern producer since he concentrated on publishing *Le Bon Ton*, a high fashion magazine featuring French fashions illustrated in beautiful color plates. Their full-size patterns were primarily available as supplements in each issue. He did limited retail sales of his patterns. Domestic used its own patterns to promote the Domestic Sewing Machine through monthly magazine and retail sales (see Figure 51).

The cost of the patterns varied, with Demorest being the most expensive. They averaged $0.25 to $0.40 each if "plain" or $0.50 to $1.50 if ordered trimmed (equivalent to $5.85 to $35.00 in 2011). Butterick averaged $0.10 to $0.30 each and $0.50 to $0.75 for complete garments, and McCall averaged $0.10 to $0.25 for complete garments. Harper's Bazar and Taylor's were free supplements with each issue of the publication. Domestic patterns were $0.15 to $0.35 for complete, sized garments.

International Companies

The success and consequential growth of the pattern industry was not confined to the United States. Promotion of patterns had begun in France and England; however, the commercialization of patterns with over-the-counter sales and mail order was essentially an American innovation, perhaps driven by the sprawling nature of the rapidly expanding country. The international pattern companies continued to thrive and expand, advertising their latest fashions in periodicals. In England, Weldon's published four magazines between 1879 and 1895. *Weldon's Ladies' Journal* carried dressmaker patterns and embroidery transfers (Adburgham 1989: 118). The company also established a Canadian edition offering patterns. Weldon's continued to grow and produced patterns into the 1950s. Beeton's included patterns in *The Englishwomen's Domestic Magazine* and in *The Young Englishwoman*. The English publication of *The Season* added over-printed pattern sheets by 1888. *The Young Ladies' Journal*, begun in 1864, produced an American edition by the early 1890s. They included pattern diagrams, a premium pattern in each issue, and a catalog of over-the-counter patterns (see Figures 52 and 53). Examples of

FIGURE 52 Young Ladies' Journal. *American edition, March 1896. Commercial Pattern Archive.*

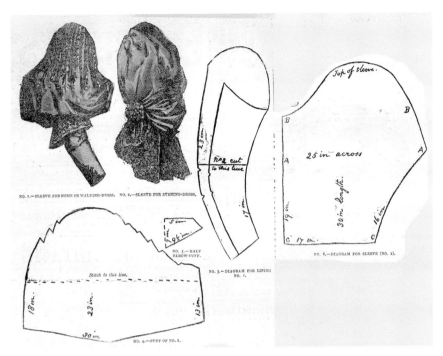

FIGURE 53 *Dress Sleeve Diagram.* Young Ladies' Journal, *American edition, November 1893. Commercial Pattern Archive.*

French publications offering patterns include *Art et la Mode*, *Le Journal des Costume*, and the long-established *La Mode Illustré*.

American presence expanded internationally. Butterick established centers outside the United States as early as 1871 with an office and distribution center in Montreal and by 1876 had offices in London, Paris, Vienna, and Berlin. Pattern prices were listed in sterling as well as dollars in *The Delineator*. Demorest established Paris and London outlets, with agents in St. Petersburg, Berlin, Frankfurt, Vienna, and Amsterdam distributing patterns sent from New York, as well as publishing multi-language catalogs (Walsh 1979: 313). Harper's was an established company with strong international ties to Berlin. Universal Pattern Company, originally Universal Fashions, began in 1881 with offices in London, Paris, and New York.

Persistent fascination with French styles was manifest. *Le Bon Ton* featured beautiful color plates of the latest fashions (see Figure 54). *Toilettes* capitalized on the fascination with the French name and specialized in Parisian designer patterns. Styles were attributed to Pingat, Doucet, and Worth among others. Unlike their competitors, they did not have agents or outlets selling their patterns (see Figure 55). The patterns were available by mail order or at the New York office. In 1897, *Toilettes'* editor acknowledged "this current age of low prices and contracted currency," citing that "many call in to their assistance paper patterns, which are well-known backers of a weak purse." They offered to ship medium-size patterns for separate garment parts (e.g., sleeve, waist, collar, etc.) for $0.10 and a coupon (*Toilettes*, August 26, 1897: 26). Normally *Toilettes* patterns were made using the customers' measurements. The patterns were expensive, up to $3.00 for a completed garment or $1.00 (equivalent to $22.60 in 2011) for separate pieces such as a skirt or

FIGURE 54 *Princess Dress $2.25, Sleeve $0.35.* Le Bon Ton, *March 1895. Commercial Pattern Archive.*

FIGURE 55 *Evening Toilette. "Models by Mason Blanche Labouvier."* Toilettes, *August 1897. Commercial Pattern Archive. Medium-size corsage with sleeve $0.75 and skirt $0.50. Cut-to-measure corsage $1.00, skirt $0.75.*

FIGURE 56 *Elizabeth Colt, ca. 1896. Courtesy of Special Collections, University of Rhode Island Library.*

bodice. (Demorest, Butterick, and McCall adult patterns were averaging $0.25 to $0.50.) Each pattern was accompanied with a small cloth model, similar to Smith's models. Mrs. Colt's sleeves in Figure 56 illustrate the popular sleeve.

New U.S. Companies and Periodicals

A serious competitor entered the pattern business in 1887. Franz Keowing was the manager of Butterick's Chicago office in the 1880s. He left over some disagreement and proceeded to open his own business, which he named the Standard Fashion Company, publishing *Ladies' Standard Magazine* to promote his patterns. In 1894, hoping to capitalize on the popular Butterick *Delineator*, he published *The Standard Delineator*. Butterick promptly sued Keowing and won, and the name changed to *Standard Designer* in 1896. The name was shortened to *The Designer* in 1898 and would not change again until 1920, when it merged with *New Idea*.

Keowing signed the major retail firm of Strawbridge and Clothier in Philadelphia to sell Standard patterns. Like his contemporaries, he sold patterns to a sole agent in a given locality. Unlike his contemporaries, he claimed that he had "the only pattern company that has always exchanged unsold patterns at cost" (Dickson 1979: 65). A fall 1894 catalog advertisement states that "Standard Patterns can be purchased from our agents in every city and town in the United States, Canada, or Mexico." Even allowing for nineteenth-century hyperbole, the company must have been doing well. The patterns were similar to what the competition was offering. The cut tissue paper had a pasted-on slip of paper containing the pattern number, size, price, illustration, and some minimal instructions. To modern eyes, the graphic style of Standard's slip of paper is more attractive than others with open space and a less cluttered look, which was achieved by printing the instructions on the back of the slip (see Figures 57 and 58).

Two other renegades started their own pattern businesses in the 1890s. J.W. Pearsall, former manager of Domestic Sewing Machine Company's pattern division, left the company to form the New Idea Pattern Company in 1894. The "new idea" was to sell patterns for $0.10 at a time when most other patterns prices ranged from $0.20 to $0.50. By April 1895, the company reported that it was cutting 1,200 to 1,500 patterns a day. New Idea patterns imitated Domestic's practice of putting patterns in envelopes with drawings of the garment and brief instructions printed on the front. There was some experimentation with the company logo before they established the official logo. A year later Pearsall began publishing *The New Idea* magazine, which was renamed *New Idea Woman's Magazine* in 1901 (see Figure 59).

The second group of renegades were Mrs. George Bladworth, editor of McCall's *Queen* under the pseudonym of May Manton, and her husband, an officer at McCall's. They left to found May Manton Pattern Company in the 1890s. Bladworth served as the company's president. Unlike most other companies, they did not immediately start their own magazine. They relied on advertising though existing publications such as *Ladies' World*, *Modes in Fabrics*, *Today's Magazine*, and *The People's Home Journal*. The patterns were titled "May Manton's Bazar Glove Fitting Patterns" using the same subheading McCall's had used in their early years (see Figure 60).

The Royal Pattern Company was formed in 1895 and began publishing *Le Costume Royal* monthly in 1896. They sold patterns in a range of sizes for $1.00 and scaled diagrams for $0.10. By 1913, they were including the "Paris Opening Models" with design attributed to Paquin, Premet, Drecol, and numerous other Parisian couturiers.

Elite Pattern Service was formed in 1897 and published *Monthly Women's and Children's Pattern Magazine*, later titled *Elite Styles*. The periodical was dedicated to fashionable women and progressive dressmakers, and it originally sold cut and punched as well as cut-to-measure patterns by mail order. By 1900 the company offered cut-to-order patterns for any garment from a mailed-in illustration. They were slow to offer a range of pattern sizes, offering only two sizes in 1920 and three in 1922. By the time the company went out of business in 1929, they were doing custom-made patterns only at $3.00 each (equivalent to $37.82 in 2011).

Pictorial Review was begun as a house organ for Albert McDowell's System of Dressmaking and Tailoring. The premiere issue, September 15, 1899, offered only one pattern, then two in each of the following months for a total of seven by year's end. The following year they offered 305 patterns. McDowell also promoted couturier patterns, which were an "exact reproduction from

No. 4809. Price, 15 Cents or 7½d.

ONE SIZE.

INFANTS' DRESS
(Suitable for christening robe)

QUANTITY OF MATERIAL:

22 inches wide..3¾ yards.
27 inches wide..3⅜ yards.
36 inches wide..2⅜ yards.

As represented, ¼ yard of tucked lawn 22 inches wide for waist, with 2⅜ yards plain lawn 36 inches wide for remainder, 4 yards of lace for ruffles, 1⅞ yards wide lace insertion to trim skirt, 2⅛ yards of narrow lace insertion to trim waist, 1⅛ yards lace to finish neck and wrists, and 3½ yards of ribbon for sash.

4809   4809

This garment may be made up in Liberty, India or China Silk, Mull, Lawn, Nainsook, Cambric or any material used for infants' dresses, and may be decorated with Lace, Embroidery, Ribbon or Fancy Stitching. As represented it is of lawn and trimmed with lace and ribbon.

No. 4809 is cut in one size.

THE STANDARD FASHION COMPANY,

NEW YORK, CHICAGO, BOSTON, ST. LOUIS, DETROIT.

CUT LABEL HERE.

PROTECTED BY LETTERS PATENT No. 371144.
NOT EXCHANGEABLE IF OPENED OR DAMAGED.
DIRECTIONS ON OTHER SIDE.   SEAMS ALLOWED.

FIGURE 57 *Infants' Dress, 4809. Standard, directions on back of label. 1899.1.JSE. Commercial Pattern Archive.*

Nos. 1519, 1033 and 1395.—Ladies' Outing Toilette.

FIGURE 58 *Ladies' Outing Toilette. Skirt 1395, $0.30; shirtwaist 1033, $0.25; and blazer jacket 1519, $0.30.* Ladies' Standard Magazine, *May 1892.* Commercial Pattern Archive.

photographs," for $1.50 ("Editorial," *Pictorial Review*, October 1900: 4). Starting a pattern company was a logical move for McDowell. His was one of the most successful of the drafting machines in the last third of the nineteenth century. However, it was considered that as good tissue paper patterns in a range of sizes became more available, dressmakers would begin to discard their drafting systems and machines in favor of buying patterns (Kidwell 1979: 101). McDowell probably saw the prospect of his market vanishing and decided to join the trend for paper patterns.

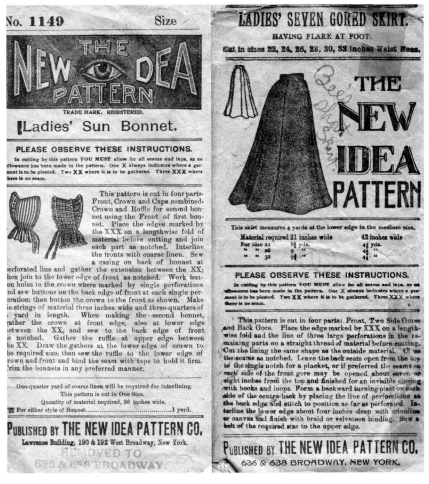

FIGURE 59 *Ladies' Sun Bonnet and Ladies' Seven-Gored Skirt. Bonnet, New Idea 1149, 1895.3.URI; Skirt, New Idea 1817, 1898.1.URI. Commercial Pattern Archive.*

One of the last companies to enter the pattern market at the close of the nineteenth century was to become one of the major companies in the twentieth century. In 1892, Arthur B. Turnurer and Harry W. McVickar, both members of New York society, decided to start a weekly gazette for the New York social set. They named it *Vogue* and heralded it as a "dignified authentic journal of society, fashion and the ceremonial side of life." Their stockholders included such social luminaries as the Van Rensselaers, Stuyvesants, Astors, Whitneys, Jays, and Mrs. Stuyvesant Fish. In 1899, Rosa Payne approached the editors of *Vogue* to suggest that they advertise a pattern she had made. The editors agreed and printed it in the February 23, 1899 issue. The pattern for the Louis XV jacket must have had a good response because Vogue continued to feature a pattern each week (see Figure 61). They were cut paper patterns that cost $0.50, expensive in comparison to other pattern company prices. They were one size only, bust thirty-six and waist twenty-four. The single sizing lasted quite a number of years. A survey of the pattern company publications

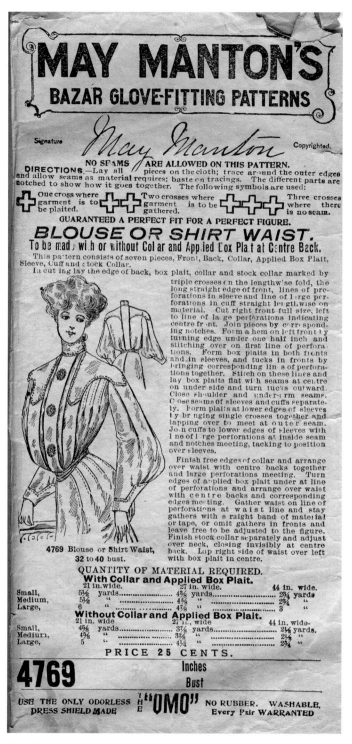

FIGURE 60 *Blouse or Shirtwaist. May Manton 4769, 1904.3.BWS. Commercial Pattern Archive.*

VOGUE'S WEEKLY PATTERN—NO. I, LOUIS XV JACKET

FIGURE 61 *Louis XV Jacket. Vogue 1*, Vogue, *February 23, 1899. Commercial Pattern Archive.*

and the new style numbers issued each year shows that Butterick issued 1,075 patterns, Standard 698, and McCall 381 in 1898; Vogue only issued one a week until Condé Nast acquired the magazine in 1909.

Summary

At the end of the nineteenth century, the home sewer and professional dressmaker had several options for creating garments. The choices were mass-produced, full-size, cut and punched commercial patterns; full-size overlay patterns such as those in *Harper's Bazar*; or patterns made with

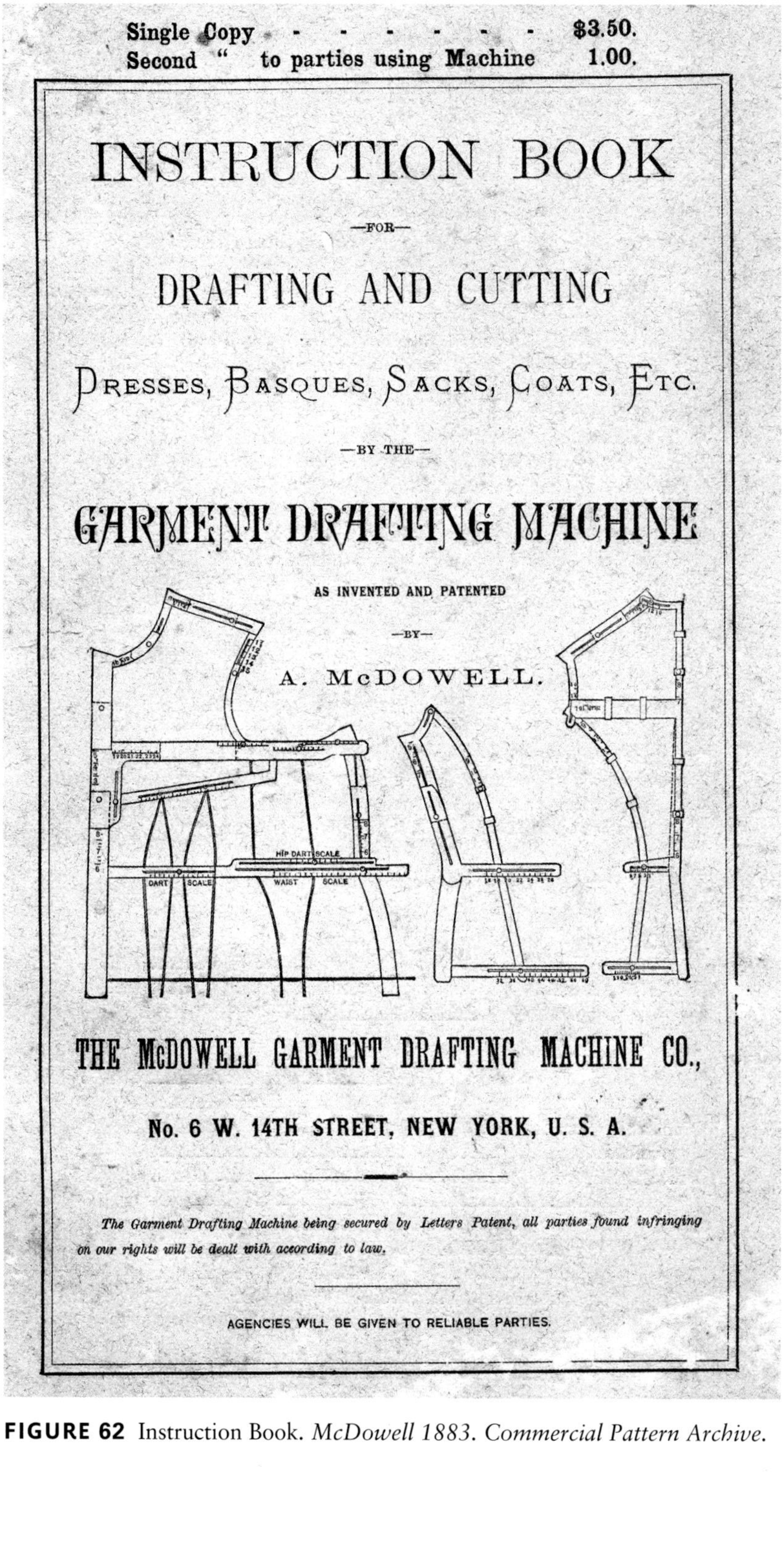

FIGURE 62 Instruction Book. *McDowell 1883. Commercial Pattern Archive.*

drafting systems. Albert McDowell was perhaps the best known for his drafting machines. He made at least five different forms of his adjustable metal machines between 1879 and 1885, with revisions through 1891 to accommodate the changing fashion silhouette (Kidwell 1979: 54) (see Figure 62). With the increased popularity of paper patterns, drafting systems were phased out after the turn of the century.

Surviving patterns and publications by the original pattern companies in the Commercial Pattern Archive and other libraries suggest the popularity of each company. Butterick, McCall, and Harper's Bazar are the most prominent. Domestic is less prominent, while Smith, Universal, and Toilettes have the lowest profile. Taylor's patterns were only included in *Le Bon Ton* and are unidentifiable when separated from the publication. Sales records for all the companies are scant; the most common source is part of company hyperbole. However, the major companies were successful enough to inspire the creation of seven new companies. These included Standard Fashion, May Manton, New Idea, Royal, Elite, Pictorial Review, and Vogue.

By the end of the nineteenth century, the pattern business had solidified. The pattern-making processes were well established. Although the designers for the patterns were rarely attributed, all U.S. companies claimed some affiliation with the latest designs from Paris; some, such as *Le Bon Ton* and *Toilettes*, attributed some of their pattern designs to specific Paris couturiers. Demorest implied that all designs were by Mme Demorest. Others, such as Butterick, McCall, and Domestic, regularly reported on the latest French fashions and relied on house designers, who were not identified, to copy them. The use of non-identified house designers was the practice well into the twentieth century.

Seemingly well-functioning companies dropped out of the competition. The main pioneer of the industry ceased producing patterns soon after the Demorests' sons took over the magazine in 1885. Domestic was phased out in 1895, as was Smith in 1897. The remaining companies and the new ones were growing, producing, and publishing patterns and periodicals. They built upon the model that evolved during the latter half of the nineteenth century to facilitate the needs of the home sewer.

6

Shifts and Balances

1900–1920s

The dynamics of nineteenth-century households shifted considerably in the closing decade. The Industrial Revolution accelerated production of ready-made garments, so clothing production in the home was less essential, minimizing the necessity of home-teaching sewing skills. Furthermore, it was more acceptable for young women prior to marriage to enter the workforce to earn an income or to get an education at one of the colleges that had begun to accept women. Thus, there was less time to devote to making clothes. In addition, department stores continued to flourish. Emerging in the 1860s, these retail establishments featured a wide inventory and were an outlet for factory-made goods. The stores encouraged the new activity of shopping, and off-the-rack clothing was a conspicuous feature of the businesses.

The changes presented a number of challenges to the twelve existing pattern companies in Table 1 and related enterprises, such as sewing machine companies, textile manufacturers, and fabric departments. In spite of this, successful new pattern companies were incorporated. In addition, a number of innovations were developed, including improved pattern-making techniques and more detailed instructions to simplify the use of patterns.

New Competition and Ventures

A dynamic new figure entered the pattern enterprise in the first decade of the new century. Condé Nast was adept at promotion and was attracted to the pattern industry. He organized the Home Pattern Company and distributed dress patterns in an arrangement with *Ladies' Home Journal* in 1905 (Seebohm 1982: 32). *The Ladies' Home Journal* was an influential women's periodical with a circulation of 1,000,000 (Mott 1938: vol. 4, 545). Nast had remarkable marketing skills and successfully promoted pattern sales.

In 1909, Nast bought *Vogue* magazine and began turning both the magazine and the pattern business into profitable operations. Prior to Nast's acquisition, *Vogue* continued to have one new pattern advertised in each weekly issue. By 1905 they were up to style number 334. Nast promoted the image that Vogue patterns were the most fashionable high styles. He had a clear vision for Vogue patterns, stating,

It is the avowed mission of *Vogue* to appeal not merely to women of great wealth, but more fundamentally, to women of taste. A certain proportion of these readers will be found, necessarily, among the less-well-to-do cousins of the rich—women who not only rightfully belong to society, but who may in fact lead very fashionable lives, and with their limited incomes, such women must look as well dressed as their affluent companions. (Seebohm 1982: 77)

Nast wanted to convince the world that Vogue patterns possessed the utmost chic in clothing styles equal to those "turned out by the famous couturiers." Further, the implication is that famous couturiers were involved, but there is no evidence of direct involvement at this time. The image created by Nast of having the ne plus ultra was established and was to endure.

Table 1   Major American Pattern Companies in 1900.

Company	Begun	Ceased
Le Bon Ton	1865	1907
Butterick	1863	
Elite	1897	1929
Harper's Bazar	1867	1913
McCall's	1871	
May Manton	ca. 1895	ca. 1922
New Idea	1896	Merged with Standard Designer 1920
Pictorial Review	1899	
Royal (Le Costume Royal)	1895	Merged with Vogue 1924
Standard Designer	1888	Merged with Butterick 1926
Universal	1888	1908
Vogue	1899	

Note: Information distilled from the Emery Papers and the Williams Papers, Commercial Pattern Archive.

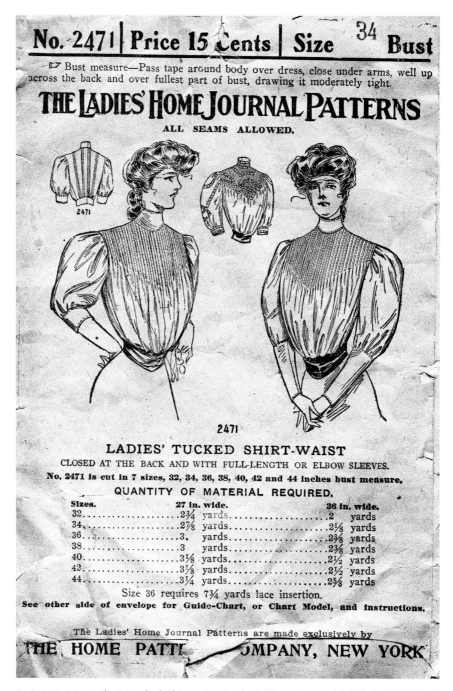

FIGURE 63 *Ladies' Tucked Shirtwaist. Ladies' Home Journal 2471, 1906.7.BWS. Commercial Pattern Archive.*

Competition and Merchandising

The home sewer had an enormous quantity of new styles from which to choose every season. A survey of style numbers advertised in the pattern company publications from 1900 to 1919 reveals that Butterick was offering between 700 and 900 new patterns each year. The Home Pattern

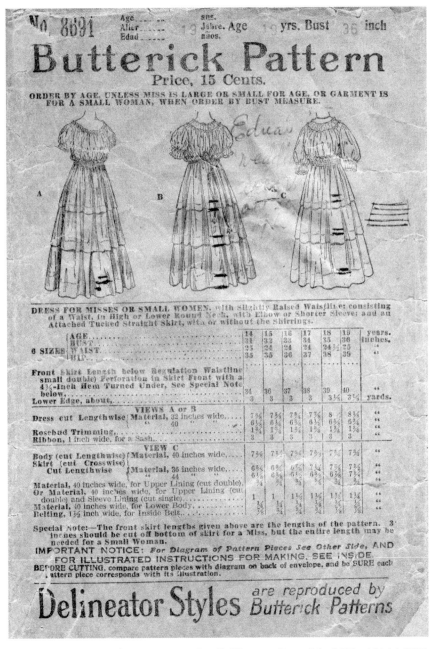

FIGURE 64 *Dress for Misses or Small Women. Butterick 8691, 1916.1.URI. Commercial Pattern Archive.*

Company issued between 400 and 500, McCall averaged 620 per year, and Pictorial Review offered from 300 to 500. Vogue continued to produce only 52 patterns per year until Nast assumed control. By 1911, Vogue was issuing over 200 patterns per year. By 1900, all the pattern companies were packaging the patterns in envelopes that included the garment design and minimal instructions. Figures 63 to 67 show a variety of pattern envelopes (see Figures 63, 64, 65, 66, and 67).

The range of garments was quite large, covering everything from elegant evening and day wear for women to work clothes and sleepwear. Children's clothes from baby layette to mid-teens as well as non-tailored garments for men were pattern company staples. Vogue was the exception. They offered very few house dresses or work clothes.

FIGURE 65 *Ladies' Tucked Waist. McCall 8563, 1909.14.URI. Commercial Pattern Archive.*

Pictorial Review Pattern

LADIES' SKIRT

With Side Plaited Flounce and Over-skirt. Closing to the Left of Center Back under Plait.

Length in front from waistline 43, back 46 inches. Width around lower edge about   yards.

Cut in sizes 22, 24, 26, 28 and 30 inches waist measure.

THE CUTTING AND CONSTRUCTION GUIDES FOR THIS PATTERN ARE INSIDE

Seam allowance on shoulders and under arm 1 inch, indicated by notches; all other seams ⅜ inch.

BE CAREFUL TO GET CORRECT SIZE. PATTERNS WILL NOT BE EXCHANGED.

Symbols Used on Pictorial Review Patterns.

Notches (V) show how the pattern is to be put together.
Large (O) perforations show how to lay the pattern on the straight of the material.
Small (o) perforations indicate lines of trimming.
Slot (▭) perforations, tucks and plaits.
One (T) and one large (O) perforation for adjusting of plaits.
Two (TT) show where pattern is to be gathered.
Three (TTT) show where there is no seam and to cut on a fold of material.
NOTE:—If any of above symbols are omitted, they are not required in the pattern.

3330

NO. OF PIECES 5.—Half this pattern is given as follows:—Yoke (A), Flounce (B), Over-skirt (C), Back Gore (D), Belt (E). Over-skirt is indicated by line of slot perforations at lower edge.

TO CUT.—Place pieces with edge marked by triple "TTT" perforations on a lengthwise fold and remaining pieces with line of large "O" perforations on a lengthwise thread of material.

TO MAKE.—Take up darts in yoke as perforated. Form plaits in flounce, creasing on lines of slot perforations, bring folded edges to corresponding lines of small "o" perforations; press to position. Join to yoke as notched.

Take up darts in over-skirt as perforated; turn hem at lower edge on slot perforations. Arrange on yoke, center-fronts and upper edges even. Form double box-plait in back gore, creasing on lines of slot perforations, bring folded edges to indicating lines of small "o" perforations in back gore, over-skirt and flounce (corresponding notches even); stitch as illustrated, leaving edges to the left of center-back free above large "O" perforation in back gore for a closing; press to position, close seam under plait. Turn hem at lower edge of skirt on double "oo" perforations.

Join belt to skirt as notched, center-backs even, leaving left side free from small "o" perforation to front edge; bind upper edge of skirt on left side.

Trim in any desired way.

MATERIAL REQUIRED

	With Nap		Without Nap
Size	54 in. wide	44 in. wide	36 in. wide
22	4¾ yds.	5¼ yds.	7¼ yards
26	4½ "	5½ "	7¼ "
30	5 "	5¾ "	7½ "

With ⅞ yard, 36 inch lining for yoke.

THE PICTORIAL REVIEW CO.
853 Broadway, New York
Price 15 Cents

FIGURE 66 *Ladies' Skirt. Pictorial Review 3330, 1909.13.BWS. Commercial Pattern Archive.*

FIGURE 67 *Ladies' Nine-Gored Kilt Plaited Skirt. Standard Fashion 8921, 1900.1.BWS. Commercial Pattern Archive.*

New Idea Pattern Company, who had built their reputation and business by selling low-priced patterns, found that other companies began to lower their prices to meet the competition. As early as 1894, McCall cut their prices to $0.10 and $0.15, and by the start of the twentieth century, Standard and Butterick patterns were selling for the same price as the other companies. In 1906, Pictorial Review patterns sold for $0.15, and the Home Pattern Company started operations with the same price. For nearly two decades, patterns remained reasonably priced, except, of course, for Vogue. In 1915 their stock patterns were priced at $0.40 and $0.50 (equivalent to $10.64 in 2011), and cut-to-measure patterns were $2.00, $3.00, and $4.00, in keeping with their image of being the most chic.

Another exception to this trend was Elite Styles Company. Their publication, *Elite Styles*, first appeared in 1897. By 1900, they were offering cut-to-measure patterns for any garment illustrated in the publication; cut tissue paper patterns were included in their offerings by 1908. However, they only stocked a medium size (bust thirty-six) at $0.15; individual cut-to-measure patterns sold for $1.00 to $1.75 or $3.00 for a complete costume. A value of $1.00 (1908) is taken as being equivalent to $20.10 (2011).

Patterns were readily available over the counter at department stores or by mail order. By around 1919, the retail stores had broken the pattern companies' insistence on exclusive contracts and could offer patterns from several different companies to customers, thus expanding their stock of patterns.

Syndicated Patterns and House Brands

Another fledgling form of mail-order patterns was advertised by pattern syndication services. These were groups who manufactured and distributed their merchandise through non-fashion periodicals and newspapers. Mostly they were sold under the name of the publication, such as *The Farm Journal*, or the newspaper that carried them, but sometimes the name of the syndicate, such as Our Own, was used. The syndicator supplied each publication with the illustration and text to the pattern department at no cost and made its money from sales of the patterns. The primary target consumer was the large rural population, specifically the homemaker and the family in the middle-income and lower bracket. For newspapers, the intent was to attract women readers to the advertising pages with the offer of patterns. According to a personal interview in 1996 with Daniel Flint, owner of Famous Features, the styles of the patterns were consciously not high-style (even "frumpy"), meant for more lasting appeal. The styles could remain in circulation for a number of years (see Figure 68).

Since they did not publish their own monthly periodicals, relying on promotions in advertising pages of newspapers and women's magazines was common practice. Syndicated companies may have begun as early as the 1880s with J. Gurrey & Company (Dickson 1979: 81). Typical examples of the syndicated pattern promotions include *Ladies' World*, which noted, "By special arrangement with the manufacturer, we are enabled to supply our subscribers patterns of all garments described on this page" (February 1893: 12). The *Woman's Home Companion* sold patterns from around 1899 through the mid-1930s, adding to the competition. *Mother's Magazine* was selling patterns from a variety of sources. In September 1907, they sold May Manton Patterns (39). In December 1908, the patterns available from the *Mother's Magazine* Pattern Department, of Elgin, Illinois, are not identified by company (54); however, pattern number 2607 for a toy rabbit is identical to Peerless pattern number C-105. Both sold for $0.10, which was the standard price for the patterns they advertised (see Figure 69).

Peerless Newspaper Syndicate (Seligman 1996: 500) was active in the 1910s. The company sold Peerless patterns though a number of periodicals, including *Mother's Magazine* and *Modern Priscilla*, as well as over the counter. The company appears to have been started by 1907 and was active through the 1930s (see Figure 70). Fashionable Dress Pattern Company, owned by the American Fashion Company, was a syndicated service that started in 1915 and lasted until 1930. They produced a wide range of patterns and published *Fashionable Dress Magazine* and *Style*.[1] Their patterns appear to have been sold only by mail order or through any of their branch offices in Chicago, Dallas, or San Francisco as well as the home office in New York, which was located in the Pictorial Review building. In the early 1920s, their patterns were selling for $0.60, slightly higher than most of the companies and similar to the Vogue prices.

Another approach to distributing patterns was taken by two major mail-order companies, Sears and Roebuck and Montgomery Ward. Sears published its first mail-order catalog in 1888.

These Farm Journal Patterns

are such a help to Our Folks that we will continue them right along. Such patterns sell in the fashion stores at from 25 to 40 cents, not one bit better, but our price is only 12 cents, including postage. For style, accuracy of fit and simplicity in putting together they are unequalled. Our Farm Journal Fair Play comes in with every order. They are positively guaranteed in every case—*a perfect fit for a perfect figure.* Full directions accompany each pattern; quantity of material given in every case. In ordering be sure to give *number* and *size* of the pattern wanted. For ladies' upper garments give bust measure; for skirts and undergarments give waist measure. For misses and children give both age and size. Children of same age vary in size. For instance—the average miss of ten years will measure 28 inches over the breast, but there are many young girls of eight years who will measure 28 inches. In such case you need a 10-year-old pattern.

Child's Dress—8128. Cut in five sizes, 4, 6, 8, 10 and 12 years.

Ladies' Blouse—8122. Cut in six sizes, 32, 34, 36, 38, 40 and 42 inches bust measure.

Ladies' Tucked Waist—8115. Cut in five sizes, 32, 34, 36, 38 and 40 inches bust measure. □ **Ladies' Three-piece Skirt—8015.** Cut in six sizes, 22, 24, 26, 28, 30 and 32 inches waist measure.

Child's Russian Dress—8117. Cut in four sizes, 4, 6, 8 and 10 years.

Ladies' Jacket—8118. Cut in six sizes, 32, 34, 36, 38, 40 and 42 inches bust measure.

Ladies' Seven-gored Skirt—8119. Cut in eight sizes, 22, 24, 26, 28, 30, 32, 34 and 36 inches waist measure.

Misses' Waist With Plastron—8125. Cut in three sizes, 12, 14 and 16 years. **Misses' Skirt.—7848.** Cut in three sizes, 12, 14 and 16 years.

Ladies' Bolero Waist—8132. Cut in five sizes, 32, 34, 36, 38 and 40 inches bust measure.

Ladies' Work or Artists' Apron—8138. Cut in three sizes, 32, 36 and 40 inches bust measure.

Boy's Nightshirt—8135. Cut in five sizes, 6, 8, 10, 12 and 14 years.

Misses' Fancy Waist—8112. Cut in three sizes, 12, 14 and 16 years.

Ladies' Tucked Shirtwaist—8124. Cut in seven sizes, 32, 34, 36, 38, 40, 42 and 44 inches bust measure.

Send a dime and a 2-cent stamp for each pattern; send another 2-cent stamp for our 4-page catalogue, showing new designs, with rules for measurement. Be careful to give size and correct measure. Keep this page for future use. Address, Farm Journal, Phila., Pa.

FIGURE 68 *Syndicated Pattern Advertisement.* Farm Journal, *December 1900. Commercial Pattern Archive.*

FIGURE 69 *Rabbit. Unidentified Syndicate pattern 2607. Mother's Magazine, December 1908. Rabbit, Peerless C-105, 1909.1.BWS. Commercial Pattern Archive.*

It is unclear when they began offering their own house brand patterns, Superior. Examples from around 1917 are in the Commercial Pattern Archive. They used several names including Economy[2] and Roebuck & Co. Patterns. The pattern name was changed to Fairloom in the mid-1940s (see Figure 71). Montgomery Ward had begun publishing catalogs in the 1870s. In 1918, they offered their own house brand pattern, Ideal. These were promoted in *The Ideal Pattern Book* as well as the *Montgomery Ward Catalog*, and some of the available styles appeared in the 1919 catalog.

Mergers and Expansion

Further business changes impacted the pattern industry. Butterick expanded by purchasing Standard Fashions in 1900 and the New Idea Pattern Company in 1902 (Dickson 1979: 86, 88). Butterick continued to run each company separately for nearly two decades. In 1919 Butterick merged *New Idea Woman's Magazine* with the *Delineator*, and in 1920, many of the pattern envelopes were printed as Standard–New Idea–Designer. The acquisition enabled Butterick to build a publication empire with three major fashion magazines: *The Delineator, The Designer,* and *New Idea Woman's Magazine.*

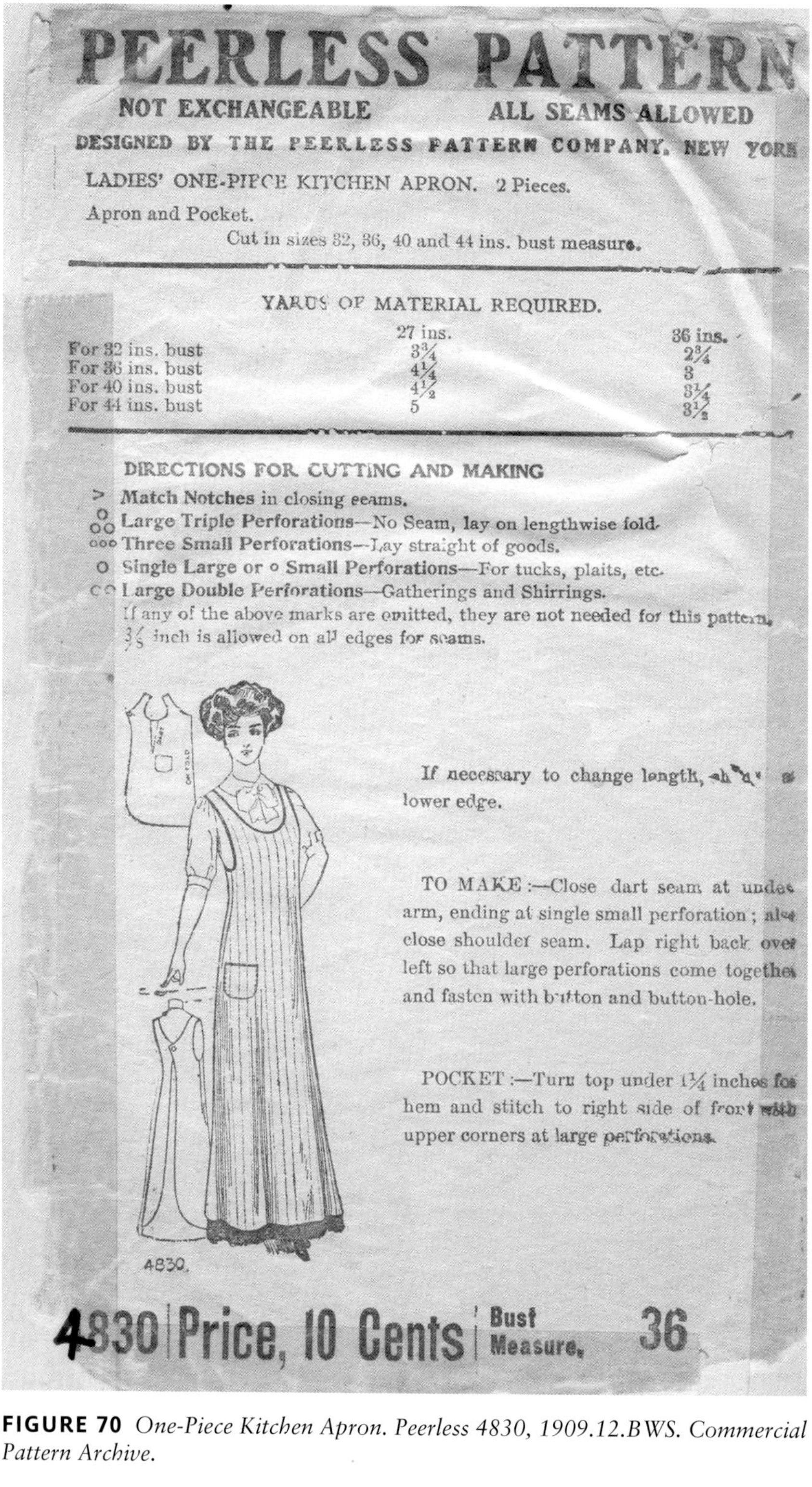

PEERLESS PATTERN

NOT EXCHANGEABLE   ALL SEAMS ALLOWED

DESIGNED BY THE PEERLESS PATTERN COMPANY, NEW YORK

LADIES' ONE-PIECE KITCHEN APRON. 2 Pieces.

Apron and Pocket.

Cut in sizes 32, 36, 40 and 44 ins. bust measure.

YARDS OF MATERIAL REQUIRED.

	27 ins.	36 ins.
For 32 ins. bust	3¾	2¾
For 36 ins. bust	4¼	3
For 40 ins. bust	4½	3¼
For 44 ins. bust	5	3½

DIRECTIONS FOR CUTTING AND MAKING

> Match Notches in closing seams.

Large Triple Perforations—No Seam, lay on lengthwise fold.

Three Small Perforations—Lay straight of goods.

Single Large or Small Perforations—For tucks, plaits, etc.

Large Double Perforations—Gatherings and Shirrings.

If any of the above marks are omitted, they are not needed for this pattern.
⅜ inch is allowed on all edges for seams.

If necessary to change length, add or lower edge.

TO MAKE :—Close dart seam at under arm, ending at single small perforation ; also close shoulder seam. Lap right back over left so that large perforations come together and fasten with button and button-hole.

POCKET :—Turn top under 1¼ inches for hem and stitch to right side of front with upper corners at large perforations.

4830.

4830 | Price, 10 Cents | Bust Measure, 36

FIGURE 70 *One-Piece Kitchen Apron. Peerless 4830, 1909.12.BWS. Commercial Pattern Archive.*

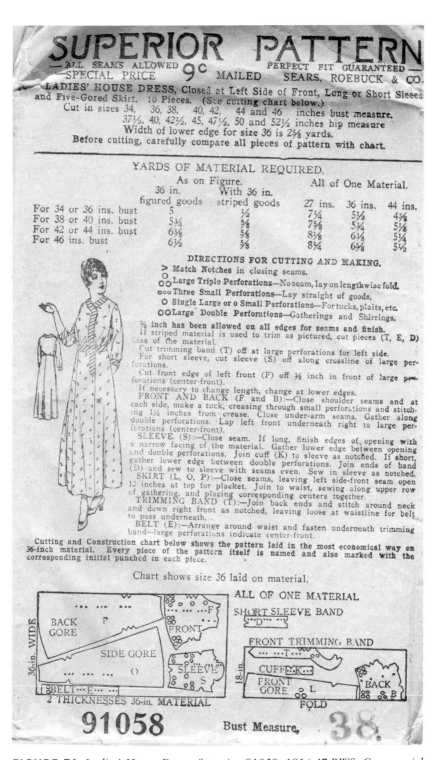

FIGURE 71 *Ladies' House Dress. Superior 91058, 1916.47.BWS. Commercial Pattern Archive.*

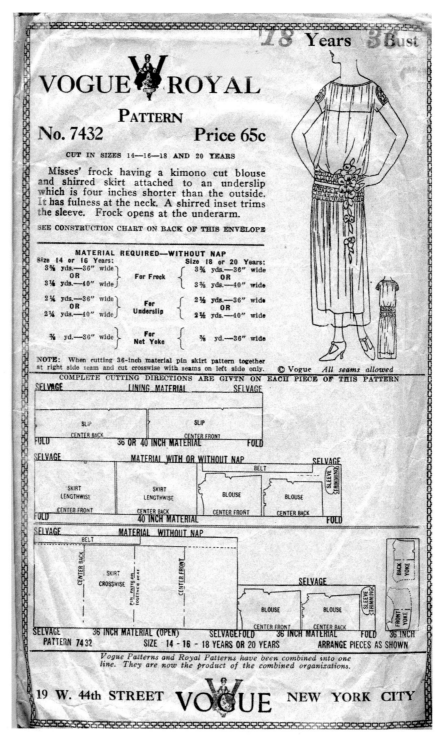

FIGURE 72 *Misses' Frock. Vogue Royal 4732, 1924.52.BWS. Commercial Pattern Archive.*

Condé Nast's enterprise acquired *Toilettes* magazine, and Peerless Pattern Company merged with Home Pattern Company in 1913. *Toilettes* was renamed *Criterion of Fashion* and advertised Home Patterns (Dickson 1979: 82). Two years later, Nast became president of Royal Pattern Company. Royal was fully merged with Vogue by 1924, when many Vogue pattern envelopes carried the "Vogue/Royal" label. By 1927 all mention of Royal was dropped (see Figure 72).

Vogue expanded its overseas market by first establishing an English distributor in 1912, then, in 1916, publishing English *Vogue*. A Spanish *Vogue* was produced in Cuba in 1918 but lasted only four years. French *Vogue* was published in 1920, and Vogue patterns could be ordered by subscribers to any of these overseas editions. Butterick published British, French, German, Spanish, Italian, and Danish editions of *The Delineator* and maintained international offices.

English Pattern Companies

Publishing and advertising patterns was different in England. Instead of individual pattern companies with their own publications as in the United States, English periodical publishing corporations produced a range of patterns, which they promoted in a variety of fashion magazines. The largest corporations include Amalgamated Press Ltd., R. S. Cartwright Ltd., Fashions for All Ltd., George Newnes Ltd., and Weldon's Ltd. There were several buyouts and mergers, so the patterns were published by different corporations between 1900 and the 1950s. The largest, most successful pattern companies during this period included Leach (1915–1935), Mabs (1917–1936, which merged with Roma in 1936), and Weldon's (1880–1935). Another popular pattern company was Harmsworth (1914–1953), which also published and sold a syndicated line of patterns as Bestway patterns[3] (Seligman 2003: 98–106). Maudella, founded in the late 1920s, was family owned and named in honor of the owner/designer, Maud Eleanor (Simplicity Pattern Company n.d.: 4).

Perfecting Dressmaker Patterns

During the first two decades of the twentieth century, patterns were still cut and punched. Each piece included a seam allowance, usually three-eighths of an inch, although larger "let-outs" were occasionally included. These were especially popular with Butterick. In general, the code was large holes punched through the tissue in a line indicated grain line, and three large holes forming a triangle indicated the edge was to be placed on a fold of material. Small holes indicate such things as fitting darts, tucks, and pocket and trim placement. Notches on the edges indicated which two pieces were to be seamed together. All the companies used a code of large and small circles. Butterick and Standard appear to have used only these, but others used squares, triangles, crosses, rectangles, and *T*s. The code was usually explained in the instructions. Patterns for ruffles were often included, but placket pieces and facings were still fairly rare.

Directions for assembling the garment continued to be minimal but began to be expanded by 1910. Envelopes became commonplace by 1910, allowing more space for directions, which were usually printed on the front of the envelope with a few small diagrams, generally for the layout of

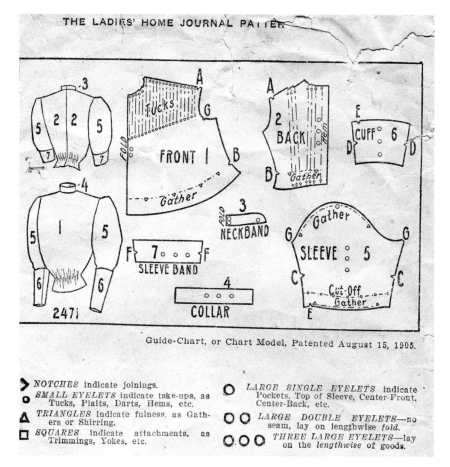

FIGURE 73 *Guide Chart, Ladies' Tucked Shirtwaist. Ladies' Home Journal 2471, 1906. Commercial Pattern Archive. (Front view see Figure 63.)*

pattern pieces for cutting. Home Pattern added a "Guide Chart" in 1905, which they patented (see Figure 73). Pictorial Review patented their "Construction Guide" in 1907, and McCall's followed suit with labeled drawings of the garment sections (see Figures 74 and 75).

The use of a separate instruction sheet was beginning. In 1909, Pictorial Review patterns carried the statement, "The Cutting and Construction Guides for this pattern are inside." This was a small piece of paper (heavier than the pattern tissue) with the line drawings of the layout of pattern pieces printed on it. Butterick was also trying to figure out how to best present their instruction information and in 1914 settled on a separate sheet of "Illustrated Instructions for Making Butterick Pattern No. _____ included in the envelope." By 1920, Butterick referred to the instruction sheet as the "Deltor," short for *Delineator,* and labeled the pattern envelope as "Butterick including Deltor." These instructions look very limited to today's consumers, but they were an immense improvement over anything that had been available previously (see Figure 76).

Standard Designer brought out "The Belrobe Method of Picture Instructions" in 1921. Of all the various instruction sheets introduced in the 1920s, the Belrobe is by far the best. The instructions are much more extensive and detailed, and there are numerous, very clear illustrations (see Figure 77).

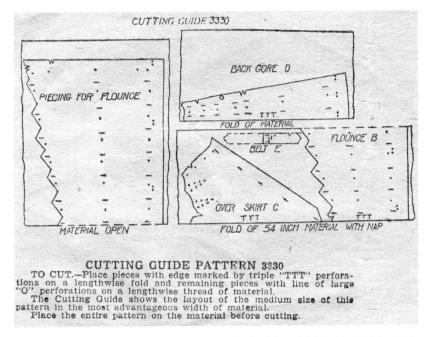

FIGURE 74 *Ladies' Skirt Construction Guide. Pictorial Review 3330, 1909. Commercial Pattern Archive. (Front view see Figure 66.)*

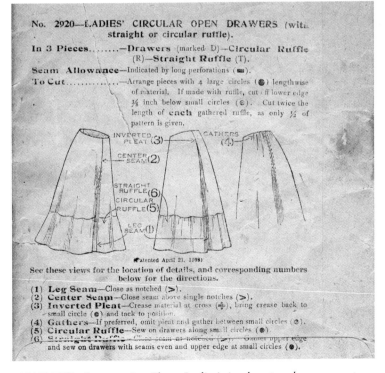

FIGURE 75 *Construction Chart. Ladies' circular open drawers construction guide. McCall 2920, 1909, 1909.1.JSE. Commercial Pattern Archive.*

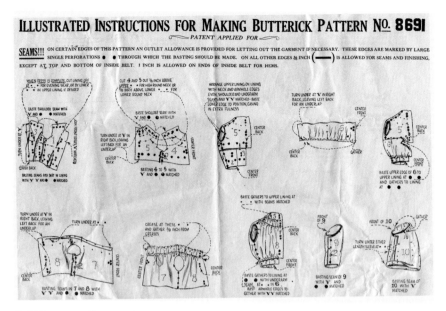

FIGURE 76 *Illustrated Instructions for Dress. Butterick 8691, 1916. Commercial Pattern Archive. (Front view see Figure 64.)*

Formal Dressmaking Programs

Family members were largely responsible for teaching the next generation sewing skills throughout the nineteenth century. But with the rise of women's education and home economics programs in women's colleges, formal classroom training became more common.[4] For women who were not able to participate in formal classroom training, correspondence courses were offered by the American College of Dressmaking in Kansas City, Missouri, under the direction of Pearl Merwin and by the Women's Institute in Scranton, Pennsylvania, under the direction of Mary Brooks Picken. Both offered highly detailed instructions for making all types of garments.

The American College of Dressmaking concentrated on drafting patterns. Their publication, *The American System of Dressmaking*, included drafts, curved rulers, and a tailor's square. The course was designed to be "a complete and comprehensive text book for the beginner, a handy guide for the seamstress at home, and a ready reference for the graduate and professional dressmaker" (Merwin 1908: preface).

The Women's Institute incorporated lessons for working with commercial patterns, tailoring garments and lingerie, and millinery, publishing a total of ninety-six books between 1915 and 1939. For *Tissue-Paper Pattern*, *Part 1* and *Part 2* (Picken 1921), they developed a relationship with several pattern companies, including Vogue, Fashionable Dress, Butterick, and McCall's, and occasionally included a tissue paper pattern with the course booklet.

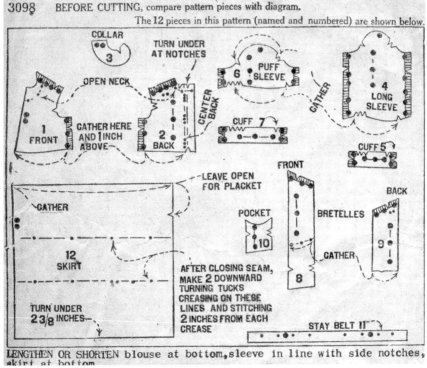

FIGURE 77 *Girls' and Juniors' Dress. Standard Designer 3098, with Belrobe Instructions, 1921.4.URI. Commercial Pattern Archive.*

Both schools established methods for reviewing samples of the student's work and responses to examination questions to judge the work for fulfillment of the degree requirements. Students worked at their own pace. The value of the Woman's Institute program was voiced by an anonymous student in *What the Woman's Institute Means to Me* (1921). The author stressed the importance of learning to sew for personal and professional advancement, savings in the clothing budget, and financial independence. The courses were updated regularly to keep pace with the changing fashions.

The pattern companies also published sewing manuals. *Butterick Dressmaker* included many editions. McCall's published *Dressmaking Made Easy* by Laura Baldt and collaborated with Emma Goodwin for *Goodwin's Course in Home Sewing*, including patterns for a woman's complete outfit, from undergarments to trimmed dress. (Patterns for the shirtwaist and seven-gored skirt are in the appendix.) Pictorial Review published *American Dressmaking Step by Step*. Additionally, the major fashion periodicals published by the pattern companies continued to include dressmaking tips in every issue.

War Efforts

With the United States' entry into the First World War, the companies rallied to the massive war effort. All responded to the call to conserve paper. The December 1918 issue of *Le Costume Royal*, for example, joined "practically every publisher" in printing no more copies of periodicals than actually ordered and to "slightly reduce" the number of designs for new pattern styles. *Elite Styles* went so far as to urge their readers to "restrict even their pattern purchases with us to the most indispensable" in response to the "grave shortage of all grades of paper" (1918: 52). Joining in the effort to conserve fabrics for the war effort, McCall's promoted the "Dress of Patriotism" in the 1918 *Book of Fashions* quarterly catalog and offered patterns for dresses that required only two yards of fifty-four-inch material for size thirty-six (*Book of Fashions* 1918: 4). Other dresses of the time were averaging three to four and one-half yards per garment (see Figure 78).

Pattern companies recognized women's participation in the war effort by providing patterns for uniforms and special work clothes. In addition to nurses' uniforms, Butterick issued the Official Yeowoman's Costume of the U.S. Navy, and McCall issued a ladies' work suit "adopted by the US Government munitions workers" (see Figures 79 and 80).

Another example of a unified effort by the pattern companies is the official uniform of the Food Administration, which was introduced in 1917 to promote conservation during the First World War. Herbert Hoover mounted the highly successful campaign that urged all conscientious women to wear the uniform to demonstrate their commitment to the program. Photographs from the period show women from all spheres of society wearing the uniform, dubbed the "Hoover Apron."[5] The apron was marketed by major pattern companies as well as being available ready-made. The universal style continued to be popular over the next decades (see Figures 81 and 82).

The American Red Cross approved garment patterns for supplying war hospitals. These patterns were sold under the American Red Cross logo as well as from the pattern companies for

This model
is cut from
ONLY
2 YARDS
of 54-inch
material

8227—LADIES'
ONE-PIECE DRESS,
opening center
front, two styles
of sleeve, attached
to dress or lin-
ing; instep length.
Pattern in 6 sizes,
34 to 44 bust
(**2 0** cents).—By
cutting according
to the diagram,
Figure I, size 36
or 38 may be cut
from 2 yards of
54-inch material.
The skirt's width
is 1⅞ yards at
l o w e r   e d g e.
Transfer Design
N o. 822 (15
cents) used on
the pocket.

Dress—8227
Sizes 34 to 44
Transfer Design No. 822

FIGURE 78 *The Dress of Patriotism: "Saving Wool for 'Over There.'"* McCall Book of Fashions, *Spring 1918. Commercial Pattern Archive.*

$0.10. Women were encouraged to make operating gowns, masks, bed shirts, robes, and bed socks. Patterns for Red Cross nurse uniforms, aprons, and veils were available from all the major pattern companies (see Figure 83). In England, Emily Peek published three books of instructions with diagrams and some loose pattern sheets for a variety of British Red Cross hospital garments, women's apparel, and knitted articles in 1914 (Seligman 1996: 123–24).

FIGURE 79 *Official Yeowoman's Costume of the U.S. Navy, 1101.* Delineator, *November 1918. Commercial Pattern Archive.*

Perhaps one of the most startling influences of the war effort for women's fashions was the acceptance of pants in the form of bloomer dresses, overalls, and service uniforms. In New York, the Female Cavalry Corps could be seen drilling in city streets in knee-length khaki riding coat and breeches, leather puttees, and brown boots "looking like some new race, neither male nor

Work Suit 8435
Small, medium, large

FIGURE 80 *Ladies' Work Suit. McCall 8435, Mc-Call's Magazine, August 1918. Commercial Pattern Archive.*

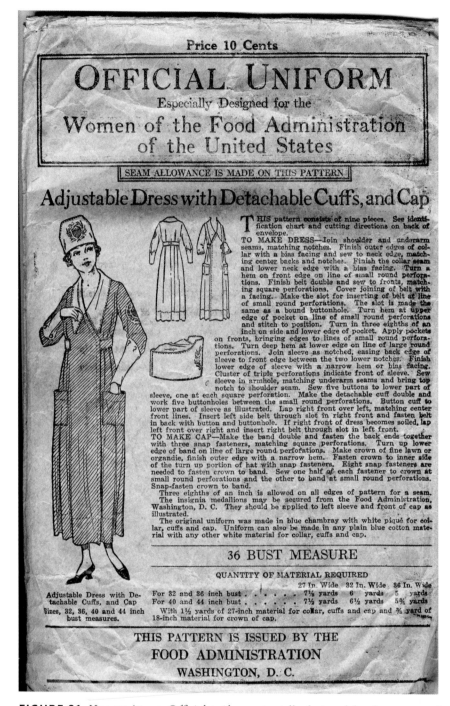

FIGURE 81 *Hoover Apron. Official uniform especially designed for the women of the Food Administration of the United States; pattern issued by the Food Administration, Washington, D.C. 1917.10.JSE. Commercial Pattern Archive.*

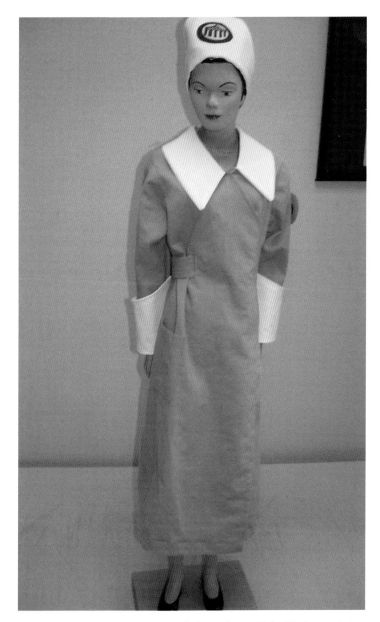

FIGURE 82 *Hoover Apron Made by Roberta Hale. With permission from Roberta Hale.*

female" (*Delineator*, August 1917: 56). A similar look was recommended of women working on "aeroplanes" or in other defense jobs usually filled by men. For women munitions workers, the official work suit consisted of a cap, blouse, and "trouseretts."

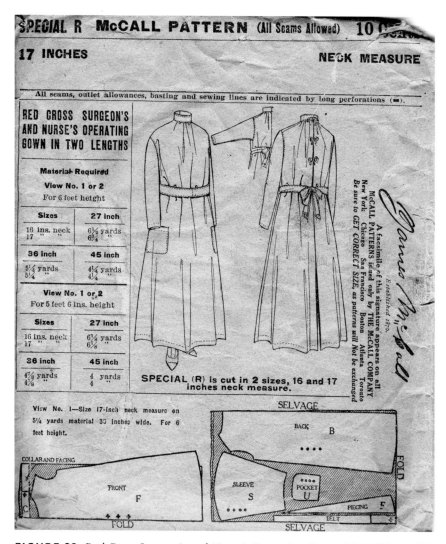

FIGURE 83 *Red Cross Surgeon's and Nurse's Operating Gown. McCall Special R, ca. 1917, 1917.9.JSE. Commercial Pattern Archive.*

Summary

The pattern companies' efforts during the opening decades of the twentieth century were concentrated on encouraging home sewers to make their own clothing. While the fashionable shirtwaist and skirt (see Figure 84), idealized by the Gibson Girl, were easy to mass-produce for ready-to-wear, patterns for each were promoted by all companies. Furthermore, the companies promoted patterns offering variety and encouraging self-expression. For example, Butterick 8691 (Figure 64)

FIGURE 84 *Shirtwaist and Skirt. Woman with hat standing by table: May Hazel Cushman Corona. Cushman Collection, 1953.70.05. Courtesy of the University of Rhode Island Historic Textile and Costume Collection.*

was individualized to make the wedding dress in Figure 85. Companies improved instructions for making a pattern and placed greater emphasis on educating women to learn better sewing skills. Pattern production methods were standardized along with improved instructions for using them. Furthermore, in addition to promoting the latest fashions, the companies' fashion periodicals were filled with dressmaking and homemaking advice in an effort to increase subscriptions and to promote the advantages and ease of making one's own clothes.

FIGURE 85 *Wedding Dress on Mannequin and Seated Woman in Wedding Dress. Dress from Butterick 8691, 1916.1.URI. Donor: Lucille Hewitt Spooner Votta, 1982.15.04. Seated woman in wedding dress: Edna Lucille Maine Spooner, married October 25, 1916, in Cranston, Rhode Island. Donor: Lucille Hewitt Spooner Votta, 1982.15.06. Both courtesy of the University of Rhode Island Historic Textile and Costume Collection. (See Figure 64.)*

The existing companies in 1900 were challenged by new competition. Home Pattern Company followed the traditional retail sales approach. Syndicated and house brand companies—such as Our Own, Fashionable Dress, and Superior—offering patterns only through mail order, were targeted to the more rural population. In the United States, mergers of pattern companies were also prevalent. These included Butterick's mergers with Standard Fashion and New Idea, Home's merger with Toilettes and Peerless, and Vogue's with Royal.

Traditions of everyday life changed dramatically during the First World War. A patriotic spirit inspired a collaborative response from all the companies, ranging from conservation of paper and materials to the production of uniform patterns for the home front and active service, and introduced a more general acceptance of women in pants.

7

Blossoming Economy

1920–1929

Postwar Effects

While the general economy was experiencing boom years in the period between the end of the First World War and the crash of 1929, not every sewing-related business benefited. Fewer women were making their own clothes or going to custom dressmakers. Since the turn of the century, an increasing number of women had been entering the workplace, and this trend continued after the war. They no longer had the spare time to lavish on making their own clothing, and the ready-made garment industry was offering well-made garments at reasonable prices from department stores and mail-order catalogs. The simple styles of the 1920s did not demand the precision of fit previously necessary, so an inexpensive ready-made dress could fit as well as one made at home or by a dressmaker. In spite of the shift away from home sewing, all of the companies from the previous decade continued to operate, with the exception of New Idea, which merged with Standard Designer in 1920; and a new company, Excella, was inaugurated in 1922.

During the 1920s, a number of factors intersected to allow more time for the homemaker. The introduction of electricity in many urban homes advanced domestic mechanical appliances to reduce time-consuming housekeeping chores. Many electric appliances patented as early as the 1890s, including the electric iron, greatly eased clothing care and garment-making chores. Washing machines, ovens, vacuum cleaners, and electric sewing machines became more common in urban homes and lessened the amount of time necessary to complete regular household chores.

Pattern companies were forced to compete with each other to attract the home sewer by making their patterns easier to use. McCall embarked on some business changes that led to remarkable growth in the next decade. In 1913 William Bishop Warner became head of the McCall Corporation. Warner's background was in merchandising, and he used that experience over a ten-year period to turn McCall patterns into a leader of the pattern industry (Mott 1938: vol. 3, 585).

Printed Patterns

McCall developed an alternative to cut and punched pattern production when they started printing patterns. They took a patent on the process and gained a big jump on the other companies.[1]

Printed patterns had the outline of the pattern piece and all other makings printed on each piece instead of punching symbols. Pattern pieces were printed on large sheets of tissue with dart placement, notches for matching the pieces together, and other pertinent information such as the name of the piece on each segment. To accommodate their overseas market, information was printed on the pattern pieces in English, French, and Spanish as early as 1926 (see Figure 86).

The New McCall Pattern, "the biggest invention since the sewing machine," was announced in 1921 (*McCall's Magazine*, January 1921: n.p.), claiming greater accuracy for each pattern since each printed piece is an exact duplicate of the original. For the instructions, McCall continued with a small-scale diagram and minimal instructions on the back of the envelope. In 1923, they introduced the *Printo Gravure*. Originally, it showed a very brief illustration of how to cut the printed pattern pieces, which had an additional margin beyond the cutting line. They began to expand the *Printo Gravure* in 1924 to large sheets with more inclusive directions (see Figure 87).

The patent was inclusive, so none of the other companies could produce all-printed patterns until the McCall patent expired. However, some companies developed creative solutions to utilize the new approach by adding some printing in their regular cut and punched tissue patterns. Pictorial Review introduced some printing by early 1925 when they added "The New Simplified Pictorial Review Printed Pattern" to the pattern envelope and the "Pictograf" instruction sheet with a cutting guide for placing the pattern on the material, a construction guide, and step-by-step directions. Announcing the superiority of Pictorial Review printed patterns, the company proclaimed "this pattern ALMOST TALKS TO YOU and answers all your questions satisfactorily and promptly." The announcement further states that "there are no misleading margins to be cut away as on other printed patterns. . . . [The perforations permit] chalking or marking of important points on the

FIGURE 86 *McCall Printed Pattern Announcement.* McCall Quarterly, *spring 1924. Commercial Pattern Archive.*

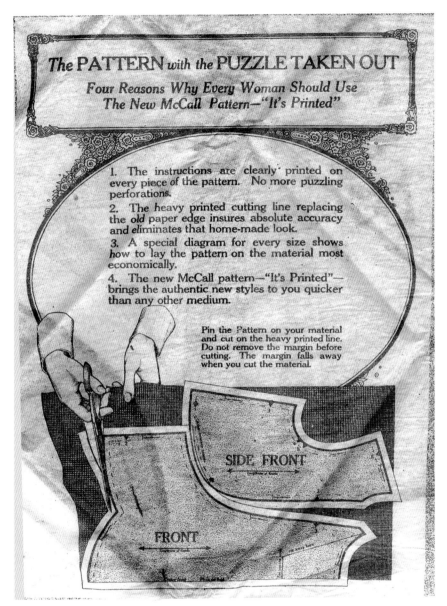

FIGURE 87 Printo Gravure. *Ladies' and misses' dress, McCall 3270, 1923.11.JSE. Commercial Pattern Archive.*

material" (Pictorial Review 1922). Pictorial Review was granted a patent for the idea in September 1925 (see Figure 88).

That same year, Excella Pattern Company also introduced a printed pattern with the Excellagraf. The format of the sheet, printed information on the perforated pattern pieces, and envelope style are very similar to Pictorial Review Patterns, which is not surprising since Pictorial Review started Excella Pattern Company in 1922 and both companies printed their patterns in the same plant. Furthermore, the two company's offices were adjoining buildings in New York City.

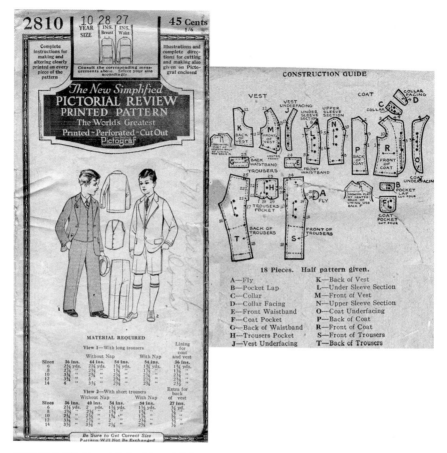

FIGURE 88 *Boys' Suit. Pictorial Review 2810, printed, perforated, cut, and with "Pictograph Construction Guide," 1925.11.JSE. Commercial Pattern Archive.*

The other companies continued with the traditional tissue patterns but concentrated on improving instructions. In 1924, Home Pattern Company announced the "Minerva Guide and Complete Dressmaking Lesson." Standard Designer, now merged with New Idea, touted their instruction sheet, the "Belrobe," for clarity and ease of use (see Figure 89). Sometime in 1922, Vogue envelopes began carrying the statement "complete cutting directions are given on each piece of this pattern" (Vogue 1922). Actually, the cutting directions consisted of a few words, such as "neck" and "lay on fold of goods" punched out in tiny holes. The rather skimpy construction guide and information chart continued to be printed on the back of the envelope, which was similar to the approach McCall had used. Vogue explored several options with their instruction formats. Some were included in the envelope; others were printed on the reverse of the envelope.

Under the creative merchandising of Warner, McCall began experimenting with color illustrations of the pattern designs in 1922 to enhance the appeal of their patterns. Early color renderings were usually reserved for transfer patterns of embroidery and other embellishments for women's and children's garments. By 1928, color illustrations were standard. In some instances the color was printed directly on the envelope; in others it was printed as a separate plate with the top edge

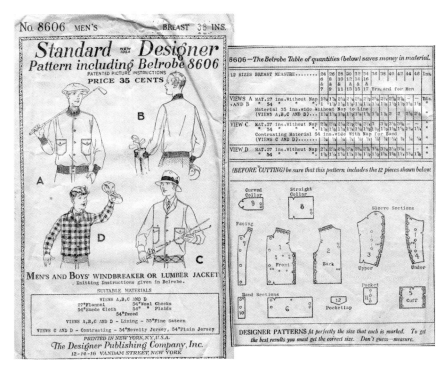

FIGURE 89 *Men's and Boys' Windbreaker or Lumber Jacket. Standard Designer combined with New Idea including "Belrobe Construction Guide" 8606, 1926.23. JSE. Commercial Pattern Archive.*

glued onto the envelope. Consequently, many of the plates have fallen off and the envelopes have survived without the illustration of the design of the pattern (see Figure 90).

Licensed Couturier Patterns

Warner also oversaw the founding of McCall couturier patterns from a wide selection of leading French houses.[2] Williams (1995) compiled her research of the McCall couture patterns for "1920s Couturier Patterns and the Home Sewer." In January 1925, *McCall's Magazine* proudly proclaimed "Paris Imports from the House of Lanvin, Chanel, Drecoll and Jenny" (61). The announcement stated that "McCall designers are continually visiting Paris where they attend seasonal openings of the greatest Parisian couturiers . . . to bring back the newest and most becoming models" (*McCall's Magazine*, February 1925: 60) (see Figure 91).

This was not a new practice. Pattern companies had been sending correspondents and designers to Paris since the mid-nineteenth century.[3] For example, *Toilettes* described their patterns as "attributed to . . . ," citing a well-known Paris couturier as early as 1881. Tailor touted his affiliation with Parisian designers in *Le Bon Ton* from the outset. The Royal Pattern Company patterns were also "attributed to . . . ." The difference with the McCall couturier patterns was the agreements

Includes printed pattern for hat in 23-inch head size, special transfer
design in yellow to fit, and photographic instructions for making
the hat step by step.
(Continued on back of envelope)

FIGURE 90 *Ladies' Hat with Transfer Design. McCall 1372, 1924.30.BWS. Commercial Pattern Archive.*

made with the Paris houses to use their models to make the patterns and to acknowledge the Paris designer in the magazine and catalog copy—and occasionally on the pattern envelope. The latter was not common practice, so a comparison of the pattern with the catalog copy is usually necessary to identify the designer.

Promoting the Parisian designers was a perfect idea for its time. The interest in and knowledge of French couture was intense and widespread. A major merchandising ploy for the entire garment industry throughout the 1920s was to make the line sound as though it were straight from Paris. Knockoffs of various Paris designers were available in every price range. In addition, a number of couturiers were designing special lines for the ready-made garment industry. McCall provided

FIGURE 91 *Ladies' and Misses' Evening Dress. McCall 5055, Design by Vionnet, 1927.197.BWS. Commercial Pattern Archive.*

everyone with the opportunity to make an authentic French couture garment. All the patterns were priced in the same $0.35 to $0.45 price range (equivalent to $4.36 to $5.60 in 2011). The strategy was to make these designs the same in quality and price as the rest of the line. The French designs amount to about 10 percent of what they had on offer.

Pictorial Review, never slow to imitate a good idea when they saw it, was offering their own French couture patterns by May 1926. Since the designs were "after" the designer, they did not have a business agreement with the designers to produce exact copies of the models as McCall did.

FIGURE 92 *Ladies' and Misses' One-Piece Dress. Paris 2243, Design by Lucile Paray and cloth label, 1933.42.URI. Commercial Pattern Archive.*

Curtis Publishing Company introduced Paris patterns in *Ladies' Home Journal* in February 1929, announcing, "Now you can reproduce exactly Gowns designed by the great dressmakers of Paris" (32). As with McCall, the Curtis patterns were licensed from leading Parisian couturiers, including designs by Worth, Dœvillet-Doucet, Redfern, Lucile, Premet, Poiret, and many others. Unlike McCall, the Paris patterns were higher in price, generally $0.65 each, than the parent Home pattern line, which sold for $0.35 to $0.50. However, Paris patterns did include a cloth label, which could be sewn into the garment when completed. Paris Pattern Company was phased out in 1933 (see Figure 92).

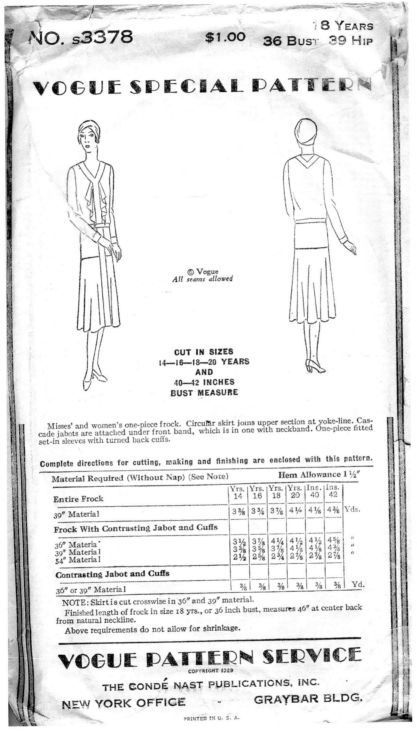

FIGURE 93 *Misses' and Women's One-Piece Frock. Vogue Special Pattern S-3378, 1929.247.URI. Commercial Pattern Archive.*

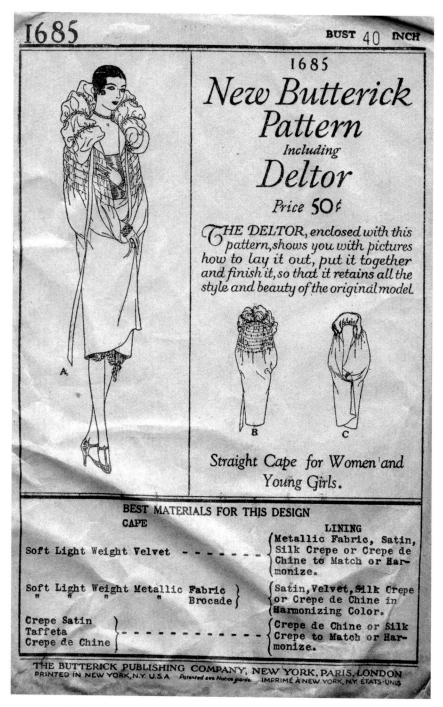

FIGURE 94 *Straight Cape for Women and Young Girls. Butterick 1685, 1927.32. JSE. Commercial Pattern Archive.*

In an effort to improve their business, Vogue began selling Vogue Special patterns in January 1927. They had a separate numbering system with an "S" prefix and cost $1.00 (equivalent to $12.62 in 2011) when regular Vogue patterns sold for $0.50 to $0.75. Other than that, there does not appear to be anything particularly special about them. No designer credit is given (see Figure 93).

Mergers

In 1920, Nast acquired *Le Costume Royal* and its pattern line, which included "Paris Opening Models," with design attributed to Paquin, Premet, and Drecol among other couturiers. In 1924 it merged with Vogue patterns. Meanwhile, as other companies were expanding and experimenting with innovations to market their patterns, Butterick merged Standard Fashions and New Idea and established two major successful fashion publications, *Standard Designer* and the *Delineator*, in 1920. They also added significant information for the home sewer when they began to include suggested materials for the patterns on the envelopes. For the rest of the decade, Butterick was under some duress and suffered considerable financial difficulties and languished.

Wilder, who had headed Butterick since 1905, had been in ill health and sold his interests in Butterick in 1926. The new owners concentrated on the financial health of the company. One of their first actions was to consolidate Standard Designer and Butterick patterns and their associated publications. The *Delineator* was combined with *Designer* in November 1926, and the Standard pattern line was dropped. In 1927, they did a major redesign of their pattern graphics and introduced "the New Butterick Pattern." However, unlike their competitors, no major changes were made to Butterick patterns. Instead, they concentrated on increasing the circulation of the *Delineator* and generating revenue from advertising in the periodical. Since the new owners had experience in publishing, coming from *Good Housekeeping*, it is not surprising that the company's emphasis was on expanding and improving the *Delineator*. They were successful. The circulation went from slightly more than a million to 200 million within two years (Peterson 1964: 165) (see Figure 94).

New Competition

A new company, Simplicity, was founded in December 1927 by Joseph M. Shapiro, a former salesman for *Pictorial Review*, and his son James J. Shapiro. It was to become one of the industry's top producers of patterns. Similar in intent to New Idea Patterns at the turn of the nineteenth century, the object was to sell affordable, inexpensive patterns at $0.15. The idea was extremely providential given the events of the crash in October 1929 (see Figure 95).

The initial production for Simplicity's patterns was begun in New York City in 1928 with an affiliated publication, *Simplicity for Smartness & Thrift*. Apparently the venture was a success because the company moved twice between 1928 and 1930, which suggests expansion. In 1930, they expanded with a Canadian subsidiary and began negotiations for manufacturing facilities in Niles,

91

SIMPLICITY PATTERN

Apron 15c

We are giving you FREE this Simplicity Pattern (sold regularly for 15c) so that you can experience the new benefits made possible only by Simplicity.

SIMPLICITY
The Only
All-in-One
PATTERN
-:-:-
Easy to Use
Economical to Buy
No Waste of
Material
Saving of Time

Designed and made by
SIMPLICITY
PATTERNS
Limited
204 King St. E.
Toronto, Ont.

Material Required: 32" Width, without Nap
(For other widths separate pattern and lay on material)
SIZE..One Size
MATERIAL..1 Yard

FIGURE 95 *Apron. Simplicity 91, 1929.110.JSE. Commercial Pattern Archive. This date is estimated and this pattern is the earliest from Simplicity in the archive.*

Michigan. The extremely popular enterprise was announced on the front page of the *Niles Daily Star* on August 26. The new industry was located in the abandoned Tower Cotton Mills and "promised to employ 100 people with a minimum payroll of $40,000" (*Niles Daily Star* 1930). The plant created much-needed jobs for the residents of Niles when it finally began production in December 1931.

FIGURE 96 *Ladies' Coat and Skirt 62311. Weldon's Pattern supplement in magazine, March, 1920.101.BWS. Commercial Pattern Archive.*

Another new company to garner a large following was Reader Mail, formed in 1927. The syndicate used the direct manufacturing method and produced house name patterns for newspapers and magazines. They manufactured patterns under several names, including Anne Adams, Marian Martin, and later Prominent Designers. They were part of the Hearst Corporation until 1987, when they were purchased by Simplicity (Simplicity Pattern Company n.d.).

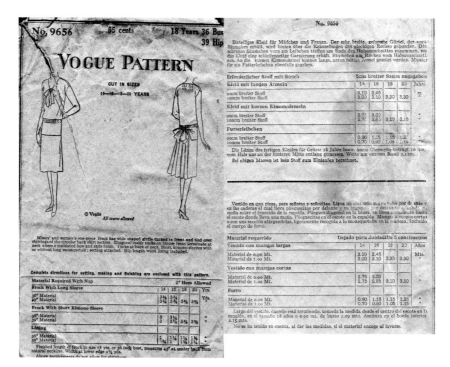

FIGURE 97 *Misses' and Women's One-Piece Frock. Vogue 9656, 1929.104.JSE. Commercial Pattern Archive. (See Figure 192 for pattern.)*

English Pattern Companies and International Affiliations

Leach-Way, the English pattern company, introduced the Sixpenny Dressmaking Series. They continued to publish the *Lady's Companion* weekly, which included a coupon for a free full-size pattern, a diagram for another outfit, and an order form for additional patterns in the publications (June 6, 1925: 142–63). Weldon continued to publish *Weldon's Ladies' Journal*, including the Canadian edition as well as the continental edition "with supplement in French, Spanish and Italian." Each issue promoted Weldon's paper patterns and included a free full-size pattern supplement along with diagrams for additional garments (1920: 1–48) (see Figure 96).

All the U.S. companies maintained offices in London and Paris. Simplicity established a Canadian subsidiary. Vogue was very active in the international scene. The British edition of *Vogue* began publication in 1916 and promoted the latest Vogue patterns. Nast also encouraged international versions of patterns such as Vogue 9656. The copy on the back of the envelope is in German and Spanish, but the instruction sheet is in English (see Figure 97).

Summary

During the 1920s, McCall was more energetic and innovative than the other six major pattern companies (Butterick, Pictorial Review, Excella, Standard, Home, and Vogue). Under Warner's direction,

McCall introduced and patented printed patterns. He oversaw the addition of color images of the styles and licensed patterns by famous Parisian couturiers. Pictorial Review and Excella adapted elements of the printed patterns, and the former marketed patterns "after" leading French designers. Curtis Publishing Company promoted Ladies' Home Journal patterns for the sizable mainstream market need for basic, serviceable garments including larger sizes for women. To tap into the demand for French fashions, they added Paris Patterns "designed by the great dressmakers of Paris" to the Home pattern line in 1929.

After a promising start at the beginning of the decade with the introduction of suggested fabrics on the pattern envelopes and the merger of Standard Fashion and New Idea, Butterick continued the middle-of-the-road course and maintained the status quo in pattern production. They consolidated each of the companies' fashion sources and marketing practices to strengthen Butterick's financial status. The company claimed production of 90 to 120 new styles per month during the 1920s (Rockwell ca. 1964: 10).[4] Vogue continued their well-established practice of promoting their patterns as the most fashionable high styles. They merged Vogue and Royal patterns in 1924 and introduced an additional line of Vogue Special Designs in 1927.

That same year a new company was incorporated and would prove to be a major competitor to the pattern businesses. Simplicity was founded with the idea of providing simple-to-use $0.15 patterns. As the name implies, the company promoted the perception that their patterns were the simplest to make.

As in all other aspects of the culture, the Depression had a big impact on the pattern companies and presented a variety of new challenges.

8

Surviving the Depression

1930s

There is a general perception that pattern companies prospered during the Depression due to the increase in home sewing. It is true that women were making more clothes for themselves and their families out of necessity. However, the pattern companies did not fare well, especially during the first half of the decade. *Business Week*, in a February 1935 article titled "Dress Pattern Progress," states,

> Pattern producers repudiate rumors that they enjoyed a boom during the Depression. Like most other businesses, theirs suffers when people are hard up; it recovers when people start spending again. Patterns hit bottom in 1932. Improvement began in the Fall of 1933, but not soon enough to make an increase for the year. Estimates place 1934 ahead of 1933 by about 10%. (*Business Week* 1935: 20)

National Recovery Administration (NRA): 1933

Some of the companies responded to government-sponsored stimulus proposals; others did not since they were not mandatory. The National Industrial Recovery Act was signed by President Franklin D. Roosevelt in 1933. It was part of the New Deal program and was, in part, an attempt to stimulate the economy and improve workers' living standards. The NRA implemented Title 1 of the act, part of which was devoted to protecting free competition, regulating working standards, and guaranteeing trade union rights. Although a code for the garment industry was formulated and officially adopted, the pattern companies were not included. However, Simplicity printed the NRA Blue Eagle symbol on their envelopes from November 1933 until June 1935, when the U.S. Supreme Court ruled Title 1 unconstitutional (see Figure 98). McCall and Pictorial Review used the symbol occasionally on flyers and catalogs but not in the patterns. Butterick and Vogue ignored the whole thing.

FIGURE 98 *Men's Bathrobe and Smoking Jacket. Simplicity 1331, NRA symbol, 1933.15.JSE. Commercial Pattern Archive.*

Finding the Market

Although a few $0.10 and $0.15 patterns were available in 1930, the average price range was $0.30 to $0.50 and chic Vogue patterns were $0.50 to $1.00 (equivalent to $16.11 in 2011). At a time when a loaf of bread cost $0.05, the price of a pattern represented serious money. Unlike the loaf of bread, however, a pattern could be used many times, shared with others, and copied, often on old newspapers. Singer's winter issue of *Smart Clothes for Fall and Winter, 1934–1935* did a cost comparison of a ready-made suit with a total cost of $29.75 to a "make-it-yourself" suit from McCall pattern 7939 for a cost of $12.41 or $4.46 with less expensive materials (*Smart Clothes for Fall and Winter* 1934: 8) (see Figure 99).

Women were sewing more, but they were buying fewer patterns and using them to the fullest extent. An alternative to a new dress was to "freshen" it with a new look by changing the sleeves or adding new collars, cuffs, or other accessories. Most of the pattern companies offered patterns with a number of sleeve styles and others with a variety of collars and cuffs (see Figures 100 and 101).

FIGURE 99 *Misses' Suit. McCall 7939. To "Make-it-Yourself," $12.41; to buy it ready-made, $29.75; to make it of less expensive materials, $4.46.* Smart Clothes for Fall and Winter *(1934).* Commercial Pattern Archive.

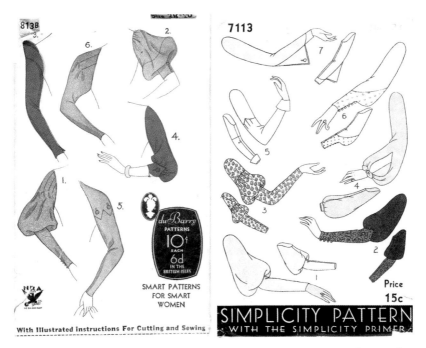

FIGURE 100 *Misses' Sleeves. DuBarry 813B, 1933.16.BWS. Set of seven sleeves, Simplicity 7113, 1932.55.BWS. Commercial Pattern Archive.*

FIGURE 101 *Collars and Cuffs. Excella E4345, 1934.25.BWS; Vogue 6614, 1934.7.JSE. Commercial Pattern Archive.*

Bad economic times or not, three new traditional pattern companies—Advance, DuBarry, and Hollywood—were launched during the Depression, and Simplicity went into full production in 1931. Shapiro, Simplicity's founder, was yet another of the merchandising geniuses who appear from time to time in the pattern industry. By naming the company Simplicity and constantly selling that idea in the catalog texts and advertising, he convinced the public that Simplicity patterns were easier to make than any other. While Simplicity patterns generally avoided the labor-intensive styles that Vogue sometimes used in their patterns, such as the intricate pleated and tucked "Dinner Frocks," other companies did as well (see Figures 102 and 103). It did not matter. Shapiro

FIGURE 102 *Evening Wrap and Dinner Frock. Evening wrap S3447 (right) and dinner frock with sunburst pleat inserts in the skirt, Vogue 5368 (left). Vogue Pattern Book, Autumn 1930. Commercial Pattern Archive.*

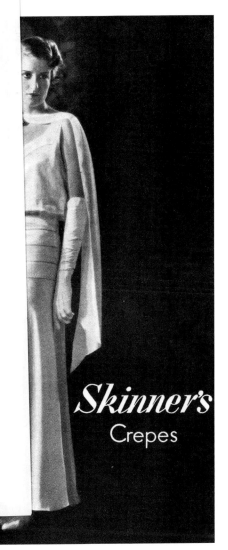

FIGURE 103 *Model Wearing Dinner Frock, with sunburst pleat inserts in the skirt. Vogue 5368 promoting Skinner's Crepes,* Vogue Pattern Book, *Autumn 1930. Commercial Pattern Archive.*

convinced the world that Simplicity was the easiest pattern to use, a perception the company has perpetuated.

Simplicity limited their publications to bimonthly catalogs including *Simplicity for Smartness & Thrift*, which became *Simplicity Pattern Magazine* in 1934. They also published *Fashion Magazine* in 1933. Perhaps the most significant merchandising idea was to offer the customer more for her money. Not only were the patterns selling for $0.15, Shapiro offered "Three patterns for the price of one. Make any or all Styles" (see Figure 104). By 1934, the company cut back to two styles per pattern, which they continued for many years. From 1934, they had two lines of pattern series,

FIGURE 104 *Top Coat in Three Styles. Simplicity 1035, 1931.18.JSE. Commercial Pattern Archive.*

FIGURE 105 *Misses' Ensemble, Frock, and Jacket. Pictorial Review 8311, 1936.50.JSE. Commercial Pattern Archive.*

the regular and Custommode. The latter was considered a more refined style and was for sold for $0.25.

In 1932, Simplicity opened a London branch and labeled the pattern envelopes "London–Paris–New York" by 1934. The February 1935 *Business Week* article reported that Simplicity claims it "ships more patterns to fill the vast chain and mail-order demands than any other company" (*Business Week* 1935: n.p.). This may have been an accurate claim. The company needed to fulfill contracts with the various pattern stores, the Woolworth network, the Kresge chain, and Sears and Roebuck.

Shapiro began negotiations with the Hearst Corporation for Pictorial Review and Excella in 1935. Pictorial Review was presenting a sprinkling of French couture patterns "adapted from" Chanel, Lelong, Patou, Schiaparelli, Vionnet, and others. Pictorial Review had begun including a Spanish-English glossary of sewing terms and some construction information in Spanish in 1932, thereby expanding the Latin American market, which made the company attractive (see Figure 105). They absorbed Excella, Pictorial's sister enterprise, in 1936 and purchased *Pictorial Review* from the Hearst Corporation in 1937. Surprisingly, it was combined with another Hearst publication, Butterick's former flagship magazine, *The Delineator* in May 1937. Both Pictorial Review patterns and the magazine were discontinued in 1939. The acquisition of Pictorial Review/Excella enterprises had an additional advantage because the companies owned equipment for printing patterns, which Simplicity did not.

In 1934, Simplicity actively engaged in a strong affiliation with the growing home economics programs throughout the country. The 1992 "Simplicity Pattern Company Chronology of Product and Events," an unpublished in-house document, reports the hiring of Caroline Hutchins (Shapiro), one of the first home economists in business, to head their Educational Division (Simplicity Pattern Company 1992). The aim was to promote home sewing skills in the younger generation with educational materials and easy-to-use patterns. The new division was an extension of the affiliations begun with the Women's Institute and the American College of Dressmaking.

New Pattern Companies: DuBarry, Advance, Hollywood

In the early 1930s, the F.W. Woolworth Co. wanted to offer a line of inexpensive patterns in their five-and-dime stores. Rumor says they approached Butterick with the idea of making a $0.10 pattern exclusively for Woolworth's. Butterick refused. When Woolworth made the same proposal to Shapiro, he agreed. The patterns, named DuBarry, were introduced in 1932. Since Woolworth's was a multination, high-volume chain, it was a lucrative account (see Figure 106).

Shapiro wasn't the only one to consider an inexpensive pattern a good idea. The Advance Pattern Company appears to have been formed by 1932 (Dickson 1979: 124). The company was affiliated with J.C. Penney Co., a chain of American mid-range department stores. Early pattern envelopes state "regular price $0.15, specially priced for JC Penney Co, $0.05." What little information that is available comes from the company catalogs, flyers, and patterns themselves. The patterns were cut and punched with minimal instruction sheets. The envelopes suggest international affiliations with New York, Paris, and London. The December 1935 *Advance Complete Counter Catalog* shows some patterns priced at $0.25 and $0.35; the special price for Penney's is not mentioned (see Figure 107).

Competition from less expensive patterns did not go unnoticed by Condé Nast. The Vogue pattern price range was $0.40 to $2.00, a steep price during the Depression, and the business was suffering. However, Nast did not want to change the Vogue image. He decided to bring out a low-price pattern line modeled after the clothes of Hollywood movie stars. In 1933, Hollywood Patterns were introduced in chain stores such as Woolworth's rivals, W.T. Grant

697

Size 16

Du Barry
PATTERNS
10¢
EACH

SMART PATTERNS
FOR SMART
WOMEN

With Illustrated Instructions For Cutting and Sewin;

FIGURE 106 *Misses' Dress with Cape Sleeves. DuBarry 697, 1932.25.BWS. Commercial Pattern Archive.*

CHILD'S FROCK and PANTIES

SIZE 4

Regular Price 15c

Specially Priced
for J. C. Penney Co.

5¢

CHILD'S FROCK and PANTIES. An
adorable model consisting of a frock and
panties. This model is very simple to
make with its pleats forming a panel effect in the front that's accented by the
novel collar detail. Note the deep yoke
across the back and the inverted pleat.
The panties are cut in one piece and
are finished with elastic at the waist.
Short cuff-trimmed sleeves add a jaunty
note. Length, size 4, 20 inches with a
3-inch hem.

ADVANCE PATTERNS

NEW YORK   PARIS   LONDON

FIGURE 107 *Child's Frock and Panties. Advance, 1931.128.BWS. Commercial
Pattern Archive. Estimated date.*

and J. J. Newberry (Figure 108). The patterns were cut and punched like Vogue patterns with small but serviceable instruction sheets. The *Hollywood Pattern Book* was modeled on the popular movie magazines, featuring articles on the stars, designers, up-and-coming films, and, of course, the latest Hollywood patterns. The implication was that the star was wearing the garment from the pattern.

JOAN BLONDELL
WARNER BROS. PICTURES

Size 18
36 Bust 39 Hip

15¢

No. 734

HOLLYWOOD PATTERN

FIGURE 108 *Misses' Overalls. Hollywood 734, 1934.33.BWS. Commercial Pattern Archive.*

Hollywood pattern styles were not of the garments worn in films, for as stated in the April/May 1935 *Hollywood Pattern Book*, "[The designs] are inspired by the clothes of the smartest stars, not copied from them. The dress which may be perfect for the camera may be too dramatic in the office or home. Our staff studies the best previews, then creates clothes in the same spirit, but easier to wear" (*Hollywood Pattern Book* 1935: 1).[1] The idea was to offer patterns for clothes "inspired by" popular films, styles the stars might wear at home or in their off-screen life. The

FIGURE 109 *Bette Davis's Bathing Suit from* The Working Man. *Designed by Orry-Kelly, Butterick Starred Patterns, Butterick B5215. Image courtesy of the McCall Pattern Company, copyright 2013.*

depiction of a "private" wardrobe featured fashions for a wide range of activities, from household chores, gardening, and sports to afternoon social activities and evening entertainment (Emery 2001: 92–99).

In 1935, *Moody's Manual of Investments* reported that Hollywood Patterns had an operational loss. But the Nast Corporation persevered, and by the end of the decade Hollywood Patterns were selling reasonably well. Butterick began making patterns for clothes actually worn by Hollywood stars in films in 1933. The first in the line featured a dress worn by Kay Francis in *The Keyhole* and two dresses designed by Howard Greer for Katharine Hepburn in *Christopher Strong*. Other patterns include a dress and bathing suit for Bette Davis in George Arliss's film *The Working Man* designed by Orry-Kelly. The venture was short-lived; Butterick's Starred Patterns series only appeared in their catalogs for a year (see Figure 109).

The Three Veterans: Butterick, McCall, Vogue

A perusal of *Moody's* from 1929 through 1934 indicates that the patterns and magazines, although hurt by the Depression, did generally show a profit. A statement in the "History of Butterick Company" claims, "In the 1930s worldwide sales of Butterick patterns attained new heights. . . . Butterick first established manufacturing centers in Toronto and London . . . a plant in Australia, and later, a distribution center in New Zealand were set in operation" (Rockwell ca. 1964: 56). The company was also making a serious attempt at less conservative merchandising with such things as the short-lived Starred Patterns. In January 1930, they announced a larger instruction sheet, the "New Deltor," with more detailed illustrations replacing the "Deltor."

However, the Butterick Company was in some financial trouble, which continued from the 1920s through the 1930s. *The Delineator* and the patterns themselves always sold reasonably well, but the company was evidently involved in other areas that lost money, and the company filed for reorganization under the Bankruptcy Act in 1935.

The company was still struggling out of bankruptcy in 1937. They sold *The Delineator*, which ranked fifth among the big-circulation women's magazines (Mott 1938: vol. 5, 400), to the Hearst Corporation. However, they established a business relationship with *Woman's Home Companion* in 1937 to compensate for the loss of Delineator pattern promotions. Some of the patterns were designated as "Companion-Butterick" patterns and carried that title on the envelopes. The relationship continued for a number of years (see Figure 110).

The exceptionally able Warner was still president of the McCall Corporation throughout the 1930s, and under his management the company rode out the Depression in excellent shape. McCall's explored new marketing ideas, one of which was reported in *Business Week*, February 16, 1935: "The McCall Company, one of the pattern leaders, recently held its own style show in New York. Languid beauties displayed 40 dresses made from new Spring and Summer patterns. Subsequently a quarter of a million housewives, patrons of 150 department stores from coast to coast are expected to view the dresses" (*Business Week* 1935: n.p.).

Warner continued to market McCall's as the "French" pattern company. The catalog offered patterns attributed to some of the top French couturiers, such as Alix, Maggie Rouff, Schiaparelli, Molyneux, and Vionnet. The entire promotional concept was summed up in their slogan, "Insist on

7586

38 BUST

45c

Frock for Shorter Women
of Larger Hip. Six-Piece
Slightly Flared Skirt.
Attached in Pointed Out-
line. Neckline in any of
Three Styles.

COMPANION ~
BUTTERICK
PATTERN INCLUDING THE DELTOR

FIGURE 110 *Frock for Shorter Women of Larger Hip. Companion-Butterick 7586, 1937.26.URI. Commercial Pattern Archive.*

a McCall Pattern—it is the shortcut to Paris Styles," which appeared on the pattern envelopes and flyers throughout the decade (see Figure 111).

In August 1932, Vogue started Vogue Couturier Patterns. Unlike McCall, Paris Pattern Company, or Pictorial Review patterns, they were not designed by or attributed to specific French couturiers

FIGURE 111 *Ladies' and Misses' Two-Piece Evening Dress and Slip. McCall 9054, Design by Molyneux, 1937.52.BWS. McCall's M 9054. Image courtesy of the McCall Pattern Company, copyright 2013.*

but were generalized "Designed in Paris" models for $2.00 (equivalent to $31.62 in 2011) (see Figure 112).

Vogue patterns were marketed in France through the French edition of *Vogue Magazine*. Nast Corporation also launched a pattern line in *Jardin des Modes*, its French-language publication, in the mid-1930s. Begun around 1920, *Jardin des Modes* offered cut-to-measure paper or fabric patterns of selected styles in the magazine. By May 1935, they dropped the cloth option and offered only regular tissue paper patterns in a range of sizes. The magazine and its patterns lasted until the German occupation of France in 1940.

FIGURE 112 *Misses' Frock. Vogue 206, Couturier Model, 1932.4.URI. Commercial Pattern Archive.*

Pattern Syndicates: New York and Famous Features

Curtis Publishing Company phased out the Home and Paris patterns by 1934. Sometime in the early 1930s, Home pattern personnel formed New York Patterns and Our Own Name Patterns. These were promoted in *Ladies' Home Journal* and were priced at $0.10 and $0.15. New York Patterns were featured in additional magazines such as *Woman's World*. *Business Week* mentioned that the New York Pattern Company "aids in private brand activity by furnishing envelopes printed with the retailer's name" (Business Week 1935: n.p.). For a brief period, around 1933–1934, New York Patterns also produced a line called Hollywood Patterns. They were not affiliated with the

FIGURE 113 *Ladies' and Misses' Tuck-In Blouse, Shorts, and Skirt. New York Pattern 220, 1935.164.BWS. Commercial Pattern Archive.*

Nast Corporation, nor did they advertise any affiliation with specific films, stars, or film designers. The line disappeared after about a year (see Figure 113). The affiliation with *Ladies' Home Journal* ended in 1936 when the magazine began showing Hollywood and Vogue patterns.

Mr. Ferris Flint founded Famous Features Syndication Service in 1932. The company produced cut and punched patterns through 1996, when the company closed. They were sold through newspapers. The house names for dress patterns included Sue Burnett, Peggy Roberts, and Ann Cabot.

The last was the house name for needlework patterns. According to Daniel Flint, owner of Famous Features, the target was the middle- and lower-income market in a full range of sizes and especially larger sizes. In its heyday, Famous Features produced two new pattern numbers a week. Numbers were consistently recycled, and popular styles could be offered for up to ten years, which makes it difficult to identify the year the pattern was issued (Williams and Emery 1996).

Summary

The pattern industry managed to come through the Depression. Only three companies had ceased production by 1939: Paris, Excella, and Pictorial Review; the latter two were taken over by Simplicity. In fact, between 1932 and 1934, three new traditional companies were formed—DuBarry, Advance, and Hollywood—as well as two newly formed syndicated pattern services. All offered patterns for $0.10 and $0.15 and filled the need for inexpensive styles. Established companies, with the exception of Vogue, did reduce prices for some patterns for a brief period.

Other than some price reduction, reaction to government initiatives during the Depression, such as the NRA, was lackluster. In response to the impact of Hollywood films during the 1930s, fashions suggesting affiliation with Hollywood starlets and actual designs by leading film designers such as Howard Greer and Orry-Kelly were made available briefly.

Marketing strategies during the decade were limited to the promotion of inexpensive patterns and photographs, rather than just fashion drawings, on models wearing the garments by Pictorial Review and Vogue. Color images to attract the customer were used by all the companies except Butterick. Some chain stores such as J. C. Penney and five-and-dime stores such as Woolworth's and Grant's established partnerships with specific pattern lines. Of all the companies, Simplicity had the greatest growth with the development of the DuBarry pattern line for Woolworth's and the acquisition and absorption of Excella and Pictorial Review.

9

The War Years

1940s

Changing Economy and International Trade

With the onset of the Second World War in Europe, prosperity began returning to the U.S. and Canadian economies. Both North and South America became major suppliers to Europe, which meant expanded production and therefore more jobs and more money for the consumer to spend. Pattern sales for all the existing companies increased noticeably, except for Butterick, which was still struggling from the problems that began in the late 1920s and were exacerbated by the bankruptcy reorganization in 1935. The 1946 issue of *Moody's Manual of Investments* reported Butterick's 1939 earnings totaled $2,252,587 but dropped to $1,876,220 in 1942 (254). Conversely, Simplicity's (including DuBarry's) net sales in 1938 were $3,649,577 and rose to $5,483,650 by 1942 (1195). McCall's sales including the magazine went from $6,363,860 in 1938 to $9,372,334 in 1942 (345).

By 1940, all the companies had increased their top prices. The U.S. government was struggling to control inflation and attempting some forced price control, first by voluntary controls and then by a campaign of persuasion. After the United States entered the war in 1941, the government established the Office of Price Administration (OPA) and imposed strict price controls. From 1941 through 1946, the top prices for patterns remained the same (see Table 2). Still, most of the companies established top prices that were high enough to carry them through the war years.

During 1939 and 1940, as the Germans overran continental Europe, more and more of the European markets were closed to the American companies. Canada and the Latin American countries provided foreign business for all pattern companies. The April 14, 1941, issue of the *New York Times* quoted Simplicity's president's letter to stockholders in the spring of 1941: "Despite current conditions abroad, your company's foreign subsidiaries showed a net loss of only $1,000 during 1940 [equivalent to $15,374.64 in 2011]. Foreign business during the period represented only nine percent of your company's net sales" (90). A large portion of the sales were DuBarry patterns (see Figures 114 and 115). His statement was probably applicable to the other major pattern companies, except for Vogue, which had a much larger commitment in France. The French edition of *Vogue* was discontinued after the German occupation, but editor Michael de Branoff "clandestinely produced Fashion Albums without German knowledge or permission" (McDowell

Table 2 Major Pattern Company Standard Prices 1940–1946.

Advance	Butterick	DuBarry	Hollywood	McCall	New York	Simplicity	Vogue
$0.15–0.35	$0.25–0.50	$0.10–0.15	$0.15–0.25	$0.35–0.50	$0.15–0.25	$0.15–0.25	$0.35–1.00

A value of $1.00 (1941) is taken as being equivalent to $15.39 (2011). Information distilled from the Emery Papers and the Williams Papers, Commercial Pattern Archive. http://www.westegg.com (accessed September 4, 2012).

FIGURE 114 *Jumper Dress. DuBarry 5235, 1941.121.BWS. Commercial Pattern Archive.*

1997: 143). British *Vogue* also experienced a setback in 1941 when a bombing raid destroyed their warehouse, resulting in the loss of 350,000 patterns and inexpensive do-it-yourself knitting leaflets managed by Harry Yoxall. Amazingly, Yoxall had duplicates of all the master patterns and one of each cutting machine for making the patterns at his home, so production was able to continue (Seebohm 1982: 351).

Paris couture had long been the major source for the American garment industry, both for design inspiration and as the arbiter of what was and was not current fashion and good taste. With Germany's occupation, the American market was cut off from French fashion news and the couture houses were struggling with a variety of restrictions imposed by the Germans (McDowell 1997: 40). It was feared this would be a serious blow to fashion in the United States. Those fears

FIGURE 115 *Jumper Dress, made from DuBarry 5235.* Singer Style Digest Fall/Winter 1941. *Commercial Pattern Archive.*

were not realized. Within a year, it was generally conceded that there were many talented American designers and that fashion would indeed survive without French input. Pattern companies turned to American designers and found that their designs sold just as well.

U.S. Government Clothing Regulations

In the summer of 1940, the American defense program got under way. Within a year a shortage of raw materials had developed. After the United States officially entered the war in December 1941, the war industries consumed even greater quantities of materials. Although the United States and Canada never had clothing rationing as they did in Britain, the governments did make attempts to regulate the situation by issuing orders to the manufacturers as well as allocating raw materials. In 1942, the War Production Board (WPB) issued Regulation L-85, specifying restrictions for every item of women's clothing. The regulation essentially froze the fashion silhouette. It limited the use of natural fibers, limited full skirts to a seventy-two-inch circumference, and banned knife pleats and patch pockets[1] (part of a "no fabric over fabric" rule). Pattern companies responded patriotically. For example, Simplicity announced "patterns with few pieces, made from 3 yards or less" in the July promotional handout flyer "Prevue Simplicity." Lingeman observes, "American fashion designers—now freed from continental influences—managed to come up with a variety of new styles and their ingenuity was stimulated rather than crippled by the restrictions" (Lingeman 1970: 125). Pattern companies were not asked to comply with the yardage limitations stipulated by the WPB. However, the companies were sensitive to the restrictions.

By February 1943, the *Journal of Home Economics* was taking a positive view. Regarding L-85, Mimi Blacker points out,

> Couched in official and technical language, the order sounds pretty formidable, but actually it did little more than accelerate trends well on the way. As long ago as September 1940, stylists forecast the return of the slim silhouette. . . . provisions in the order are generous enough to permit infinite variety in design. . . . in practice it, like fabric limitations, is resulting in better styling. (Blacker 1943: 74)

Restrictions on yard-goods were of major importance to the home sewer. Blacker continues, "The needs of the armed forces and Lend Lease[2] requirements have first call on the stock of raw fibers as well as spinning and weaving equipment of the country. . . . The headlines tell the story in a curt 'Fabrics Limited to Staples—Few Novelties woven.'" Blacker defines fabric staples as materials "we return to again and again because of their inherent good qualities" and concludes that the real title could be "Fabrics limited to Favorites" (1943: 73–74). In another section of the February issue, the *Journal of Home Economics* reports, on a less upbeat note, that retail stores were experiencing occasional shortages of even rationed fabric, and the practice of textile manufacturers attempting to increase their profits by lowering the quality of both fabric and dyes continued. Pattern companies addressed the shortage with patterns promoting the use of scraps of material left over from other garments.

It might be assumed that wartime paper shortages and allocations of wood pulp would limit the amount of paper patterns being manufactured and sold. This does not appear to have been the case. The article "Susie Sews" in the June 13, 1942, issue of *Business Week* stated,

The sale of patterns increased 25 percent last year—more than double what it was in 1940. Low-priced Simplicity patterns ($0.10 and $0.25) which account for more than half of total volume reported a 36 percent increase last year, and evidence that the boom hadn't reached its peak is provided by a report of McCall pattern sales in the month of February: up 58 percent. . . . an estimated 65,000,000 dress patterns were sold in the US last year—one for every woman and girl-child in the country." (*Business Week* 1942: 58)

However, in 1943, *Business Week* noted, "There's just one thing that now threatens to stem the flood of sewing—a War Production Board order stopping sewing machine production." Singer responded by slowly selling its stockpile of machines and cashing in on "the big needlecraft boom by selling instruction [in their stores] instead of machines" (*Business Week* 1943: 68). Further, Singer Sewing Machine Company estimated that there were twenty-five million sewing machines in U.S. homes (almost ten million more than telephones in the home). Singer stated that "a well cared for sewing machine is somewhat longer lived than an elephant" (*Business Week* 1943: 71).

Women and War Work

With the United States' entry into the war, many of the larger companies immediately published patterns in association with the American Red Cross for the home front, POWs, refugees, and hospitals (see Figures 116, 117, and 118). They also produced patterns for women's nursing uniforms and related service work. In 1942, Butterick offered a nurse's uniform and an American Red Cross Volunteer Special Service Corps uniform.

Women were recruited for factory work to replace the absent men and needed appropriate clothing. Allis Chalmers and Sperry Gyroscope Co. commissioned well-known designer Vera Maxwell to design a jumpsuit for their female factory workers as depicted in the famous Rosie the Riveter "We Can Do It!" poster. Simplicity pattern 4104 bears a strong resemblance to Maxwell's design, as does Advance 2913, designed by the Bureau of Home Economics (see Figures 119 and 120). Women in pants (trousers) were not considered acceptable as they were generally considered unfeminine; however, necessity began to change their acceptability for women during the war.

The patriotic spirit that pervaded the United States is reflected in the patterns, especially in McCall's 1943 Victory Apron 1090 with this ditty (see Figure 121):

Tie this apron round your waist
And join the Victory war-on-waste;
Plan your meals for zest and vim
And don't forget Ye Vitamin!
Remember that the right nutrition
Is Uncle Sam's best ammunition!

FIGURE 116 *Optional List of Advance Patterns Selected as Types for the American Red Cross. Advance Patterns, December 1941. Commercial Pattern Archive.*

FIGURE 117 *Women's and Misses' Frock or Nurses' Uniform. Butterick 1900, 1942.59.BWS. Commercial Pattern Archive.*

FIGURE 118 *American Red Cross Volunteer Special Service Corps Uniform. Butterick 1906, 1942.60.BWS. Commercial Pattern Archive.*

FIGURE 119 *Misses' and Women's Slack-Suit or Coverall. Simplicity 4104, 1942.106.URI. Commercial Pattern Archive. (See Figure 196 for style 2 pattern.)*

FIGURE 120 *Misses' Blouse and Jumper Slacks. Advance 2913, 1942.72. URI. Commercial Pattern Archive.*

FIGURE 121 *Ladies' and Misses' Victory Apron. McCall 1090, 1943.154.URI. McCall's M1090. Image courtesy of the McCall Pattern Company, copyright 2013.*

FIGURE 122 *"V for Victory Dress" in Women's and Misses' Sizes. Simplicity 4084, 1942.74.URI. Commercial Pattern Archive.*

FIGURE 123 *Doll's Outfit. Coverall and cap, Red Cross apron and scarf, dress, and party dress. McCall 1015, 1942.170.BWS. Commercial Pattern Archive.*

FIGURE 124 *Peggy, the Modern Fashion Model. Booklet for Peggy, the Modern Fashion Model, McCall, 1942, and Peggy in nurse's uniform, McCall 6600–1, 1942.64.JSE. Commercial Pattern Archive. Uniform made by Roberta Hale, with permission from Roberta Hale.*

In the same spirit, Simplicity issued the "V for Victory Dress" in 1942. The embroidery transfer for the pocket is included in the pattern (see Figure 122). Butterick added WACs', WAVES', and nurses' uniform patterns to their Jr. Miss Manikin doll line of patterns; McCall issued a doll wardrobe that included coveralls and a Red Cross Nurses' uniform and head covering (see Figure 123) as well as a fashion doll, Peggy, and a pattern for a nurses' uniform (see Figure 124). Simplicity also did patterns for accessories such as the "War-Plant Hat," day hats, handbags, mittens, and gloves (see Figure 125). Vogue did not include patterns specifically designated for uniforms or factory work but did include a few women's trouser patterns and some accessory patterns.

Make and Mend

In order to conserve scarce raw material, the federal government urged the women of America to "use it up, wear it out, make do or do without." The Spool Cotton Company published *Make and Mend for Victory* in 1942. The contents range from mending, patching, creative use of scraps of fabric, yarn, and cotton to converting men's suits and shirts for women and children to

FIGURE 125 *"War-Plant Hat Is Made of One Bandanna." Simplicity 4700, Simplicity Catalog, November 1943. Commercial Pattern Archive.*

reclaim used wool, touting the idea that "There's Life in the Old Girl Yet" (*Make and Mend* 1942: 43) (see Figure 126). Pattern companies responded by offering patterns to "Reclaim worn, out-moded dress" (Simplicity), "Restyle the top of that tired, old dresses" (McCall), and make "[s]omething new from something old" (Butterick). Vogue did a few makeover patterns,

There's Life in the Old Girl Yet

1. Jerkin From Dress (Advance 5047).
2. Jumper From Dress (Hollywood 499).
3. Jacket From Dress (McCall 4764).
4. Playsuit From Dress (Simplicity 3392).
5. Weskit From Jacket (Butterick 2098 or DuBarry 5416).

10. Bathing Suit From Dress (Simplicity 3885 or DuBarry 5372 for Shorts, Simplicity 3164 or Du-Barry 5439 for Top).

6. Bolero and Skirt From Coat (Simplicity 4221 for Bolero, 3885 for Skirt). 7. Daytime Dress From Evening Dress (Simplicity 4221). 8 and 9. Pinafores From Dresses by Cutting Out Sleeves and Underarm Sections.

FIGURE 126 *"There's Life in the Old Girl Yet."* Make and Mend for Victory. *Commercial Pattern Archive.*

including one for a women's jacket and skirt from a men's suit and makeovers for a boys' suit as part of the children's pattern series (see Figure 127). Patterns for collars, cuffs, and other makeover accessories as well as sleeves for remodeling dresses were readily available. Dickeys to wear with jackets instead of blouses became popular. Further, matching brother/sister outfits could be made from out-of-style adult clothing.

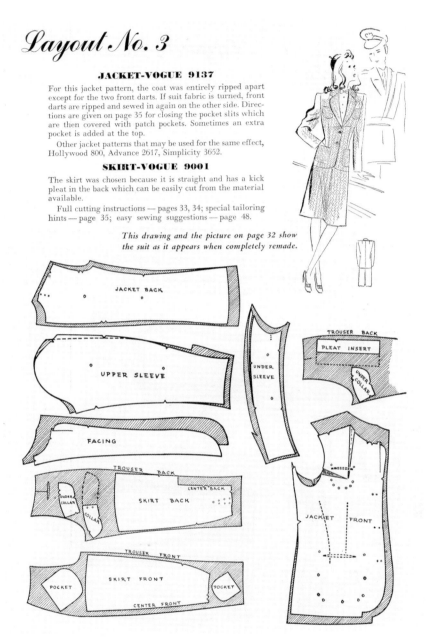

Layout No. 3

JACKET-VOGUE 9137

For this jacket pattern, the coat was entirely ripped apart except for the two front darts. If suit fabric is turned, front darts are ripped and sewed in again on the other side. Directions are given on page 35 for closing the pocket slits which are then covered with patch pockets. Sometimes an extra pocket is added at the top.

Other jacket patterns that may be used for the same effect, Hollywood 800, Advance 2617, Simplicity 3652.

SKIRT-VOGUE 9001

The skirt was chosen because it is straight and has a kick pleat in the back which can be easily cut from the material available.

Full cutting instructions — pages 33, 34; special tailoring hints — page 35; easy sewing suggestions — page 48.

This drawing and the picture on page 32 show the suit as it appears when completely remade.

FIGURE 127 *Layout 3 Jacket and Skirt. Vogue 9137 and Vogue 9001.* Make and Mend for Victory. *Commercial Pattern Archive.*

Singer Sewing Machine Company published *Make-Over Guide* in 1942 and 1943, concentrating on the same topics as well as lingerie and household furnishings. In addition, the U.S. Department of Agriculture issued a series of "make-overs" leaflets. The 1942 leaflet No. 230 is "make-overs from men's suits" and included instructions for a boys' jacket, a girls' coat, a women's jumper, and women's suit and jacket (see Figure 128).

I'm Wearing Dad's Old Suit

Companion Reader-Reporter Virginia Scholz tells how she made this good-looking new suit from her dad's old one. Total cost: $4.16.

FIGURE 128 *Makeover Suit. Using Butterick 2470,* Woman's Home Companion, *April 1943. Commercial Pattern Archive.*

In Britain, the incentive was "Make-Do and Mend" personified by Mrs. Sew and Sew, a cartoon character. Clothing rationing in Britain began in 1941. A range of utility clothing was introduced as part of the "fair shares" policy because of the shortage of fabric. The restrictions were similar to the "L" restrictions adopted later that year in the United States. The "Make-Do and Mend" policy was encouraged as a means of adjusting to the effects of rationing with the same approach as "Make and Mend." A rash of how-to booklets covered topics such as remaking garments from old, mending, patching, and darning and stimulated the growth of Make and Mend classes in schools as well as evening classes for women (Reynolds 1999: 331).

U.S./British Patterns

Pattern companies on both sides of the Atlantic responded to the needs of these consumer restrictions. American companies continued to sell patterns in Britain throughout the war. The headline in a 1941 Butterick Company in-house newsletter, "Bombs Fall Over London—Butterick Carries On," probably held true for other major companies. Comparison of American, Canadian, and British patterns shows that the designs and numbering are identical. The noticeable

FIGURE 129 *Junior Miss Princess Jumper, Beach or Sports Frock. Butterick 1093, 1940.22.BWS. British release with purchase tax. Commercial Pattern Archive.*

FIGURE 130 *Misses' and Women's Blouse and Skirt. Simplicity 1056, 1945.95.URI. Commercial Pattern Archive. British price 1s. 6d.; "Professional dressmakers are reminded that they must comply with the making of civilian clothing (restriction) orders."*

differences between British wartime pattern envelopes and those sold in the United States during the same period included the lack of color on the British pattern envelopes, price in shillings and pence, and British purchase tax stamp. The purchase tax, introduced in October 1940, was usually 16 percent (McDowell 1997: 81) (see Figure 129). Pattern companies were attempting to

FIGURE 131 *Jumper Suit. Bestway C20996, 1945.92.URI. Commercial Pattern Archive.*

meet the British government's wartime restrictions. In 1942 and 1943, Simplicity printed the government warning, "Professional dressmakers are reminded that they must comply with the making of civilian clothes (restriction) orders" on the envelopes of both Simplicity and DuBarry British patterns (see Figure 130).

British pattern companies included Bestway, Maudella, and Weldon's (which also advertised syndicated companies). Paper Patterns Ltd. changed its name to Style in 1940 and introduced Economy Patterns (Seligman 2003: 97) (see Figure 131).

Utilize and Conserve

The practice of utilizing scraps while extending the wardrobe led to the practice, and fashion statement, of piecing different fabrics together. For example, many patterns show blouses, jackets, and dresses with contrasting collars and sleeves (see Figure 132). To highlight this fashion, *Life Magazine*, on April 12, 1943, featured a dress designed by Hattie Carnegie, which retailed in her New York salon for $175.00 (equivalent to $2,288.45 in 2011). In a partnership with Simplicity,

FIGURE 132 *Two Fabric Jackets. Butterick 3084 and 3087 leisure or sports jacket, 1944.97.URI and 1944.187.URI. Butterick B3084. Image courtesy of the McCall Pattern Company, copyright 2013. Butterick B3087. Image courtesy of the McCall Pattern Company, copyright 2013.*

FIGURE 133 *Misses' and Women's Dress. Simplicity 4688*, Simplicity Catalog, *1943. Commercial Pattern Archive.*

the design, pattern 4688, was available for $0.15 (equivalent to $1.89 in 2011). The appeal of the design, with yoke and sleeves of one material and waist and skirt of another, was that it could be kept looking new and fresh by making a new yoke and sleeves (*Life Magazine* 1943: 51) (see Figure 133).

The need to conserve and "make do" accelerated home sewing instruction. "The Pattern Industry's Place in the War-Time Economy" (McCall Pattern Co. 1943), an unpublished McCall's study, reports that the U.S. Office of Education study of 14,000 high schools found over 10,000 sewing courses were being offering in 1940 and that four million girls were enrolled in sewing classes (10). The author gathered the information from "Sewing Success" (1943) in *Business*

Week. McCall's initiated the "Sewing Corps," a series of six lessons on basic sewing, given as free handouts by department and fabric stores. In 1942, Butterick published *School Book* with over 100 pattern styles twice yearly. The patterns were suitable projects for school sewing classes. The book provided spaces for local merchants to paste in fabric swatches. Butterick also sponsored school fashion shows in key cities. Simplicity had set an example in 1934 when they organized the Education Division with Caroline Hutchins as director. By 1937, Hutchins edited "School Sewing Service News" for high school sewing teachers and continued as editor of *Modern Miss* when it replaced "School Sewing" in 1940.

All of this developed the rise of the teenage girl as a separate market in the 1940s. Patterns were specifically designed to have a "teen look." The concept of the teenage market originated in the 1930s with Butterick's "younger looking fashions" and Junior Miss patterns and was fully

Table 3 Size Comparison: Teen, Misses, and Junior Miss, Simplicity 1943.

Teenage					
Sizes	10	12	14	16	
Bust	28	30	32	34	
Waist	24	25	26	28	
Hip	31	33	35	37	
Misses					
Sizes	12	14	16	18	
Bust	30	32	34	36	
Waist	25	26.5	28	30	
Hip	33	35	37	39	
Junior Miss					
Sizes	9	11	13	15	17
Bust	27	29	31	33	35
Waist	23.5	24.5	25.5	27	29
Hip	30	32	34	36	38

Note: Information distilled from the Emery Papers and the Williams Papers, Commercial Pattern Archive.

accepted in the early 1940s. Simplicity promoted "Trendy Teen" styles; Advance included teen styles from the late 1930s and promoted them for classroom sewing. Measurements for specific sizes were essentially the same as the sizing in previous decades but were now designated for junior miss and teenage, as seen in the comparison sizing chart in Table 3.

FIGURE 134 *Misses' Suit and Blouse. Vogue 1051, Paris Original designed by Schiaparelli, 1947.147.URI. Vogue V1051. Image courtesy of the McCall Pattern Company, copyright 2013.*

End of the War

At the end of the war, restrictions on clothing were lifted in the United States. Materials available to the home sewer gradually increased and the interest in making clothes for self and family carried over into peacetime. With inflation affecting all areas of the economy, home sewing was an effective cost-saving activity. Many women found their efforts resulted in better quality and fit than off-the-rack garments.

With the Liberation of Paris, leading Paris couturiers, anxious to reestablish the Paris fashion industry and raise money for war victims, created *Théâtre de la Mode* in 1945. Composed of exquisitely clothed twenty-seven-inch dolls dressed by leading couturiers and placed in elaborate settings created by such artists as Jean Cocteau and Christian Bérard, the *Théâtre de la Mode* toured major cities in Europe and the United States. French couturieres successfully reaffirmed their influence in the fashion industry. Vogue gradually began to identify some Paris designers in their Couturier pattern series in 1947 (see Figure 134). However, American designers had achieved more recognition during the war and continued to produce designs for the retail market and the pattern companies. But American designers were not credited by the pattern companies until Advance established the American Designer series in 1950.

Summary

The dynamics for pattern companies shifted considerably during the Second World War. While the economy improved after the Depression, resources for fashion designs, available materials, and government restrictions affected all of the companies. Furthermore, pattern exports shifted from occupied Europe to the Western Hemisphere. In response to these shifts, pattern companies encouraged alternative fashion design from many (often unidentified) American designers. Restrictions on raw materials and regulations on the use of fabric in clothing created a need for new styles. The restrictions led to the promotion of conserving materials and encouragement of home clothing production through such programs as "Make and Mend" in the United States and "Make-Do and Mend" in Britain. The companies continued their efforts in home sewing education in secondary schools as well as in the home. A new market for teens coincided with the emphasis on sewing education in secondary schools.

After the long years of war, austerity, and deprivation, a change of sprit, expressed in fashions, was eagerly anticipated. Paris wanted to recapture its lead in the fashion industry with the *Théâtre de la Mode* exhibit and the exuberant fashion ideas displayed. Just as the pattern companies had adjusted to the economic influences of the Depression and then the war years, they now faced the challenges of a peacetime economy and reactive new fashions.

10

Shifting Trends

Postwar–1950s

Rationing in the United States was terminated by 1945 except for sugar and rubber tires. However, it continued into the early 1950s in Britain. Regulation L-85, intended to conserve materials, was lifted in 1947. The British equivalent, CC41, remained in effect until 1954. With the restrictions lifted, more fabric could be used so garments could be fuller and longer than during the war, as adroitly capitalized upon with Christian Dior's New Look in 1947. The war had effectively shut down communication with the French fashion industry, but alternative fashion resources quickly materialized and the American style emerged as a major influence, especially for the sportswear and casual wear that came to epitomize the American woman. The new styles also promoted youth and teenage fashion.

In the United States, major population shifts were under way. The expansion of factories producing materials to support the war resulted in the influx of workers from rural to urban areas. After the war, these workers and returning veterans continued to congregate in urban centers and required housing. As a result, suburbs expanded and new ones were built to meet the demand, which introduced a new middle-class culture. Families had accumulated savings during the war years and were able to purchase new homes, cars, and other items and indulge in leisure time and family activities such as the backyard barbecue.

Selling women on the necessity of returning to the role of homemaker was a priority after the war. Advances in various new appliances such as washing machines and other household equipment that eased time-consuming chores were promoted to make the transition more attractive. All were advertised in women's magazines and the rapidly expanding mass media of television. Images of the "ideal" family were exalted in the increasingly popular television medium in such programs as *Father Knows Best* and *Leave it to Beaver*.

Pattern designs for aprons epitomize the push to revert to women's role as homemaker in the postwar culture. While patterns for utilitarian aprons continued to be offered, fancy, frilly hostess or cocktail aprons became popular for the suburban housewife placing emphasis on leisured, middle-class pursuits such as afternoon luncheons and cocktail parties. Barbecue aprons for the suburban male supported that new leisure pastime image (see Figures 135, 136, and 137).

Women were expected to spend a great deal of time in the kitchen and doing other housekeeping duties. Advertisements for new household appliances reinforced postwar depictions of homemakers wearing the latest fashions and hose and heels. If an apron was shown it was usually frilly.

FIGURE 135 *Apron and Potholder. Advance 5727, 1951.8.JSE. Commercial Pattern Archive.*

FIGURE 136 *Women's and Misses' Reversible Holiday Apron. McCall 1822, 1953.264.URI. McCall's M1822. Image courtesy of the McCall Pattern Company, copyright 2013.*

FIGURE 137 *Mr. and Mrs. Aprons. McCall 1319, 1947.88.URI. McCall's M1319. Image courtesy of the McCall Pattern Company, copyright 2013.*

The New Look

The exuberance at the end of the war was expressed by the Paris fashion designer Christian Dior. His New Look in the Spring–Summer 1947 collection is described as a sea change in fashion and had a marked impact on women's postwar styles (see Figure 138). Anticipating freedom from the fabric restrictions imposed by rationing during the war, Dior emphasized a large bust, small waist, below-mid-calf-length full skirt, and a full peplum emphasizing the hips. The style became immensely popular. However, the change was so fast and startling, it took some time for the fashion industry to adjust. Of course, there was the question of whether the style would catch on or if it

FIGURE 138 *Junior Two-Piece Suit. McCall 7060, English price 2s. 6d., 1947.70.JSE. McCall's M7060. Image courtesy of the McCall Pattern Company, copyright 2013.*

was to be a short-lived fad. The May 12, 1947 issue of *Life* magazine asked the question, "Skirts: Up or Down?" (99). Consider the trauma and consternation created by the rapid acceptance of the New Look in early 1947.[1]

Designing and making patterns, developing related advertising, copyrighting, and printing had to be done several months in advance to get the new catalogs and patterns to the stores at the appropriate time. By that time, the spring/summer catalogs and patterns would already be in the

FIGURE 139 *Junior Miss and Misses' Two-Piece Dress. Simplicity 1866, 1946. 214.BWS, and Simplicity 1866, revised in 1947. Commercial Pattern Archive.*

stores and the fall line would be nearing completion. The pattern companies had to scramble to keep up with the new fashion. Since the new fashion had the greatest impact on women's street dresses and suits due to narrower shoulders, wider hips, and longer skirts, new patterns for these garments were required. In some cases, minor changes to already existing patterns could be made as illustrated by Simplicity number 1866, first issued in 1946 and reissued in 1947 with a longer skirt. (The fastest and simplest solution was to lengthen existing skirt patterns by three inches.) Butterick offered options for remaking or altering existing garments to meet the requirements of the new style with skirt flounces, added hip yokes, or detachable peplums in 4408 (see Figures 139 and 140).

Existing Pattern Companies

When the war ended, five major companies were producing patterns: Advance, Butterick, McCall, Simplicity, and Vogue. All were moderately healthy, with good pattern sales and—with the exception of Advance, which had no self-promoting fashion magazine—reporting good income from their fashion publications. Modes Royal, a sixth company, had begun in 1943 and was producing patterns into the 1960s. The syndicated companies including Famous Features and Reader Mail continued to have strong, popular sales. DuBarry, Hollywood, and Peerless pattern companies all closed by the end of 1947 (see Figure 141).

The U.S. economy at the end of the war was strong because of accumulated savings. Even though ready-to-wear was readily available and affordable, many women did continue to make

FIGURE 140 *Set of Yoke, Flares, and Flounces for Skirts. Butterick 4408, 1948.53.URI. Butterick B4408. Image courtesy of the McCall Pattern Company, copyright 2013.*

garments for themselves. *Simplicity Pattern Book* editor Virginia Hale reported in the February 23, 1951 issue of *Time* that a recent survey showed that "her reader is probably married, has children and is still young enough to have a pretty good, manageable figure. Best of all, about one out of four garments she owns she made herself" (52).

No. 680   Size 18

A
MODES ROYALE
"Customized"
PATTERN

PRICE.
$2.00

MODES ROYALE -- PATTERN DEPARTMENT
253-255 Seventh Avenue   New York 1, N. Y., U.S.A.

FIGURE 141 *Misses' Dress with Halter or Yoke Top. Modes Royal 608 and envelope, 1949.239.URI. Commercial Pattern Archive. Date of 1949 in archival number is estimated.*

To retain their customers and attract new ones, the companies pursued several campaigns. All except Vogue continued supporting sewing programs in the high schools and, in affiliation with Singer Sewing Machine stores, aggressively promoted their products to the teenage market. The companies all expanded teen pattern styles (see Figure 142).

When McCall's patent for printed patterns expired, the other companies began to convert to printed patterns, although the question of whether printed or cut and punched patterns produced the most accurate results continued to be debated. Simplicity began to convert to printed patterns in 1945; Butterick began printing some patterns in 1950. Advance and Vogue began printing some patterns later.

The companies accelerated the use of named designer patterns. Vogue led the way with the Paris Original series in 1949. Unlike the Vogue Couturier series, the designer was identified and Vogue entered licensing agreements for the use of original models or *toiles* from Paris couturiers for duplication in their patterns (see Figure 143). As with the Couturier line, woven cloth labels were included in the pattern envelope. Simplicity quickly followed Vogue's approach with their Designer series, which had a top price of $0.50 in comparison to Vogue's $2.00 price. However, the Simplicity designer was not identified. In 1949, Advance established a partnership with the

FIGURE 142 *Dress or Jumper, Blouse, and Cape. Teenage fashions, Advance 4808, 1948.92.URI. Commercial Pattern Archive.*

New York Times for a "Designs of the Times" American Designer series featuring up-and-coming young designers such as Jerry Silverman, Herbert Sondheim, Adrian, and Anne Fogarty (see Figure 144). Butterick and McCall occasionally featured designer patterns, and Reader Mail introduced the Prominent Designer series in the mid-1950s (see Figure 145).

Sizing of the patterns continued much as it was in the 1930s with some refinement, such as the introduction of the teen sizes in the late 1930s. Simplicity added toddler sizes for six months to four years old. The measurements were the same as those for boys', children's, and girls' patterns from previous years. Sizes ranged from six months to sixteen years. Simplicity expanded again in 1958 with the sub-teen size range of patterns.

FIGURE 143 *One-Piece Dress. Paris Original designer Paquin. Vogue 1057, 1949.188.URI. Vogue V1057. Image courtesy of the McCall Pattern Company, copyright 2013.*

Standard measurements for pattern sizes were not necessarily adhered to. The companies used flexible measurements for the sizes, usually within a one-half- to one-inch variation. Proportional relationships of bust/chest to waist and hips were generally the same. In the 1940s, bust-to-waist was between five and five and a half inches and bust-to-hip three inches. During the 1950s, with the change in silhouette, the bust-to-waist ratio was adjusted to seven to eight inches with a bust-to-hip ratio of two inches.[2]

FIGURE 144 *Misses' Bra, Blouse, and Skirt. Advance 5558, American Designer Series, designer Mildred Orrick, 1950.174.URI. Commercial Pattern Archive.*

ORIGINAL
by
Philip Hulitar

PROMINENT AMERICAN DESIGNER

A896- SIZE

FIGURE 145 *Misses' Dress. Prominent American designer Philip Hulitar, A969, 1951.468.URI. Commercial Pattern Archive. Date of 1951 in archival number is estimated.*

The Great Depression and the war years witnessed the end of the pattern company monthly fashion magazine publications with the exception of *McCall*. The periodical title was changed to *McCall's* in 1951 and continued to feature new patterns until 1974. Butterick and Simplicity limited their publications to quarterly pattern books. Simplicity published *Simplicity Pattern Book* and changed the title to *Simplicity Fashion Magazine—for Women Who Sew* in 1954. All the major companies published large counter catalogs for the retail market.

New Company

In 1950, James Spadea founded his own pattern company after Butterick turned down his proposal to offer fashionable signed originals by famous-name designers. Spadea offered designer patterns for $1.00. (Vogue Couturier patterns were $2.00, but Advance was selling American Designer Patterns for $0.50.) Spadea's patterns were syndicated and originally sold through 21 newspapers, expanding to over 300 and more than 850 department stores by 1962. The original seven designs by seven famous American designers grew to a collection of 700 original designs by eighty-three well-known American and European designers. Spadea reinforced the affiliation with haute couture by cutting the patterns to "designer measurements, not standard pattern measurements." The scale was also in keeping with ready-to-wear sizing standards. Patterns were cut and punched rather than printed, which was the practice with most syndicated companies. This method allowed for short runs of the patterns and greater flexibility in producing a variety of styles. In 1959, Spadea negotiated with the Duchess of Windsor to design an exclusive separate collection. Two years

FIGURE 146 *Afternoon Dress. Duchess of Windsor Pattern, Spadea 1, 1959.61.JSE. Commercial Pattern Archive.*

Spadea with the Duke and Duchess of Windsor attends a showing of the Duchess's styles at a New York department store. Under her contract with Spadea the Duchess's designs are sold only in pattern form.

FIGURE 147 *Spadea with Duke and Duchess of Windsor. At the New York showing of the Duchess's designs. T. Howard (1962),* Saturday Evening Post. *Commercial Pattern Archive.*

later, he collaborated with singer Dinah Shore to design a "Wonder Wardrobe" of six patterns as an all-purpose travel ensemble. The set sold for $4.00 and was bought by 135,000 women by 1962. The family-owned company prospered through the 1950s and into the 1970s (Howard 1962: 36) (see Figures 146 and 147).

Feedbags

In an overview of the postwar years, it is easy to overlook the rural population since there was so much activity in other strata of society. However, the pattern companies aggressively courted this market. The syndicated pattern companies continued to market through local newspapers and farm periodicals. One long-standing practice of thrift and fashion was the use of printed cloth bags used for seed, feed, and bulk household products such as flour. The bags were made of cotton or rayon in a variety of printed percales, chambray, denim, and similar fabrics suitable for garments. The bags were a popular source of materials from the 1930s until replaced by cheaper paper bags in the 1950s. The National Cotton Council published several booklets on the use of feedbag garments. After the Second World War, Simplicity increased their affiliation with the National Cotton Council to promote pattern styles suitable for the bags. The patterns specified the size and number of bags required for each garment (*Ideas for Sewing with Cotton Bags* 1955: 2) (see Figures 148 and 149).

FIGURE 148 *"Daytime Wear."* Needle Magic with Cotton Bags *(1950), Memphis, TN: National Cotton Council. Courtesy of the National Cotton Council.*

FIGURE 149 *Women's Dress. Simplicity 3440, 1951.179.BWS. Commercial Pattern Archive. "Can be made from cotton bags."*

Summary

The end of the war brought many changes. In the United States, the shift from rural to urban and then to suburban life accelerated. When rationing was lifted, austerity was replaced with energetic consumer consumption. For many there was greater prosperity due to the accumulated savings enforced by lack of available goods during the war years. Fashion reflected the resurgence of a more romantic, feminine fashion look instigated by Christian Dior's New Look, introduced in February 1947 (see Figures 150 and 151). The feminine role of "Rosie the Riveter" changed to the happy homemaker with a more feminine silhouette, full bust, cinched-in waist, and full skirts supported by stiffened petticoats and crinolines. New leisure clothing was introduced with Bermuda shorts, pedal pushers, capri pants, variations on halters and bare midriffs, and two-piece swimsuits, as

FIGURE 150 *Misses' Coat Dress. Simplicity 8451, 1951.14.URI. Commercial Pattern Archive.*

well as the bikini. The introduction of casual sportswear was inspired by emerging American fashion designers and had an international impact, ultimately leading to the acceptance of women in trousers outside the factory (see Figure 152).

Pattern companies responded quickly to these changes and initiated some of their own, including greater emphasis on patterns designed by leading Parisian and American designers. They

FIGURE 151 *Misses' Coat Dress.* Modern Miss,
Winter 1951. Commercial Pattern Archive.

encouraged new consumers in the teenage market with special designs, promotion of sewing classes, and advertising in new periodicals devoted to the teen market, such as *Seventeen*.

Five companies—Advance, Butterick, McCall, Simplicity, and Vogue—dominated the market and were joined by Spadea featuring named designer fashions and an affiliation with the Duchess of Windsor.

By the end of the 1950s, the "idealized" suburban lifestyle promoted throughout the decade began to crumble. New energies, influences, and technology initiated restructuring and revised focus for the pattern industry.

FIGURE 152 *Junior Miss and Misses' Tapered Pants, Boxy Tops. Butterick 7557, 1955.64.BWS. Butterick B7557. Image courtesy of the McCall Pattern Company, copyright 2013.*

11

New Challenges

1960s–1980s

Boom Years

A common misconception is that by the 1960s women stopped sewing and making their own clothes due to the mass of inexpensive, readily available ready-to-wear options. However, the 1960s were actually a boom period. The *Barron's* article "Profitable Patterns" (1958) reported that pattern companies were generally profitable, with the exception of Vogue. The parent company, Condé Nast, was publishing several magazines and running the pattern division, which operated at a loss. However, the losses "are expected to be transitional due to the expensive changeover" from cut and punched patterns to printed patterns begun in 1956. Within a few months, pattern sales increased after the first phase of the changeover and the company was operating in the black (*Barron's* 1958: 9).

Figures for all pattern sales were estimated to be $50 million in 1961. Butterick, McCall's, Simplicity, and Vogue garnered the bulk of the income, followed by Advance, Modes Royal, and Spadea (*Barron's* 1962: 11). Aggressive sales approaches prompted the volume. Butterick began selling patterns in major chain grocery stores such as A&P, Stop & Shop, and Safeway. Equally aggressive merchandising expanded the overseas market. Simplicity, for example, was printing patterns in English, Swedish, Dutch, and Japanese and completed a new plant in Hatogaya, Japan, in 1961 (Hobby 1964: 9–10).

Dynamic marketing was highly successful in the 1960s. Examples include Simplicity's advertising campaign featuring the celebrity model/actress Suzie Parker proclaiming "If I Can Sew, You Can Too." Ease of use and patterns for garments that could be made quickly became a hallmark for all the pattern companies except the high-style Vogue. Simplicity, Butterick/Vogue (Butterick and Vogue merged in 1961), and McCall were dubbed "The Big Three." They all utilized TV advertising by sponsoring programs. McCall's gave a grant to National Education Television for a 1963 program series, "Smart Sewing Lessons." All provided free professional services to the five million students in 50,000 schools throughout the country. According to Joan Greene, reporting in *Barron's*, the home sewing market consisted of over forty million individuals who averaged twenty-seven garments per person each year. Further, four out of five teenage girls were making their own clothes. Clearly the persistent appeals to teens in the school programs, in TV advertising, and with the ease of sewing were successful. Affiliated businesses aligned with the successful market. Sewing machine sales were profitable, as were the proceeds from fabrics and notions (Greene 1967: 11, 19).

Furthermore, the price of ready-to-wear skyrocketed in the 1960s due to inflation, steeper transportation costs, and higher wages. *Forbes* reported that a simple ready-to-wear dress might cost $18.00 in 1961 (equivalent to $136.00 in 2011) but $35.00 in 1971 (equivalent to $186.29 in 2011). Compare that to the cost of a pattern, fabric, and notions, and the home sewer could have a dress for around $12.00 (*Forbes* 1971: 43). The summer 1967 issue of *American Fabrics* stressed the growing appeal of sewing to express individuality and as mark of elegant economy (1967: 65).

New Sizing

Pattern companies had been using the same measurement system for their patterns since 1930, when the U.S. Bureau of Standards set measurement and sizing standards for pattern measurements in response to complaints from consumers. These were based upon anthropometric measurements taken by a group of home economists (Dickson 1979: 113). The need for standardized sizing was twofold. Prior to the 1930 standards, the companies used their own set of measurements so there was no consistency. From the beginning, misses' sizes were based on age and women's sizes based on torso proportions. A size 14 was designated for fourteen years of age with a thirty-two-inch bust; size 18 was for eighteen years of age with a thirty-six-inch bust, all for an average height of five foot three to five foot four. For women, the size was based upon the bust measurement: if the bust measured forty inches; the size was 40. Relationships of bust to waist and hips changed with the changing styles of undergarments and shifts in acceptable physical activity for women, but the designated size remained.

In response to numerous complaints about the discrepancy between standard ready-to-wear sizing and pattern sizing, measurements for the new sizing were developed and approved by the Measurement Standard Committee of the Pattern Fashion Industry. "New Sizing" was introduced in 1967. Misses' size 14 was recalculated for a thirty-six-inch bust for an average height of five foot five to five foot six; women's size 40 was for a bust measurement of forty-two inches. Men's and children's sizing remained the same; children's continued to be based on age and men's were based on the chest measurement.

In efforts to provide well-fitting patterns, most companies offered as many as thirteen different choices by the 1960s: Misses, Women, Half-Size, Junior Miss, Junior Petite, Teen, Sub-teen, Chubbie, Girls, Children, Toddlers, Boys, and Men. One exception was Vogue with five: Misses/Women, Junior Misses, Teen, Proportional, and Men. Spadea used designer measurements and limited their offerings to Misses, Women, and Men. Another tactic, begun in the mid-1970s, was to combine two to three sizes in one pattern, allowing the seamstress to mix and match sizes appropriate to an individual's measurements (see Figure 153). In 1978, metric units of measurement became standard. Pattern manufacturers in the United States as well as those based in Britain and Europe began including both units of measure on their patterns.

Table 4 New Sizing Sample Chart.

	Misses 1966	1967	Women 1966	1967
Size	14	14	40	40
Bust	32	36	40	44
Waist	26	27	34	36
Hips	35	38	43	46

Note: Information distilled from the Emery Papers and the Williams Papers, Commercial Pattern Archive.

FIGURE 153 *Misses' Shirt-Jacket or Shirt, Top, Skirt, and Pants. McCall's 4587, 1975.318.URI; three sizes in one. McCall's M4587. Image courtesy of the McCall Pattern Company, copyright 2013.*

Changing Fashions: Youth Explosion

Major cultural changes were under way during the 1960s. In reaction to the perceived constraints of 1950s values, a youth-based counterculture emerged with a distinct impact on fashion. In contrast to the popular, demure Chanel suit and shirtwaist dresses favored by the previous generation, the new fashions were bold statements expressing new freedoms and ethnic influences in exuberant, often psychedelic colors. New synthetics such as polyester and single, double, and bonded knits were especially suited for the new styles. The new fabrics were wrinkle-free, stretchable, easy to work with, and did not require ironing (see Figure 154).

Hemlines climbed to mid-thigh thanks to British designer Mary Quant's miniskirt in 1965. The influence was not dissimilar to the impact of Dior's New Look in 1947. The consternation over the acceptable, fashionable hem length was repeated, but this time there were four different lengths: the mini, the regular, the midi, and the maxi lengths. *Life Magazine* pinpointed the dilemma with the feature "The Midi Muscles In," noting that many women were taking evasive actions, often selecting pants or pantsuits rather than choosing a skirt length. In the world of the movies and TV, designers and producers were again using half-shots from the waist up or filming girls in pantsuits rather than risk being out of step with fashion by the time the film or program was aired (1970: 24–27). The pattern companies solved the dilemma by offering as many as four different skirt lengths in a single pattern plus pants in many instances (see Figure 155).

A wide variety of styles ranging from hot pants, hip-huggers, and bell-bottom pants to wrap dresses (made famous by Diane Von Furstenberg) and decorative vests fulfilled the desire of the

FIGURE 154 *Fabric Swatch, Psychedelic Colors.* American Fabrics, *Winter 1968.* *Commercial Pattern Archive.*

FIGURE 155 *Misses' Skirts in Four Lengths: Mini, Regular, Midi, and Ankle. Simplicity 7725, 1968.279.URI. Commercial Pattern Archive.*

home seamstress to create her own individual look. The new relaxed styles spilled over into men's garment patterns as well. In addition to body shirts, hip-huggers, and bell-bottoms, less structured, unlined jackets and suits were popular and easier for the home sewer to make than lined, tailored garments. Patterns for leisure suits, three-piece suits, and various sports jackets were manufactured (see Figure 156).

The new fashions reflected the unisex movement promoted in the late 1960s and 1970s. Pants, especially the new hip-hugger bell-bottom pants, and pullover tops were adopted by men, women, and children. Loose-fitting ethnic-influenced styles such as robes, caftans, and vests were readily adopted for casual wear by both sexes (see Figure 157).

FIGURE 156 *Men's Body Shirt and Bell-Bottom Hip-Hugger Pants. Simplicity 8255, 1969.13.JSE. Commercial Pattern Archive.*

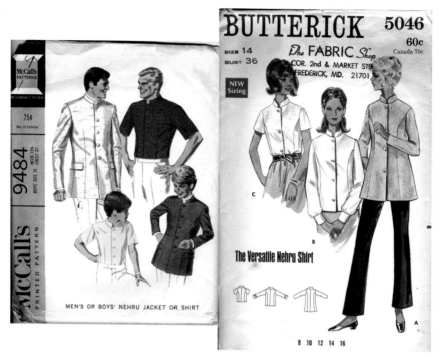

FIGURE 157 *Men's or Boys' Nehru Jacket or Shirt and Versatile Nehru Shirt. Nehru jacket, McCall's 9484, 1968.477.URI. Nehru Shirt, Butterick 5046, 1968.653.URI. McCall's M9484. Image courtesy of the McCall Pattern Company, copyright 2013. Butterick B5046. Image courtesy of the McCall Pattern Company, copyright 2013.*

FIGURE 158 *Misses' Jacket or Vest, Blouse, Skirt, and Pants or Shorts. New Sizing Butterick 5375, 1969.469.URI. Butterick B5375. Image courtesy of the McCall Pattern Company, copyright 2013.*

Pattern companies were quick to respond to the changing market with several strategies. All introduced pattern lines that offered patterns for a full wardrobe of blouse, skirt, pants, and jackets in various lengths and slightly different styles (see Figure 158). Advance affiliated with film and TV celebrity Loretta Young for a line of special designs in 1961. By 1965, Butterick arranged licenses for the Young Designers Series with new designers including London designers Mary Quant and Jean Muir, and McCall offered the New York Designer collection featuring designers such as Rudi Gernreich, Bill Blass, and Pauline Trigere (see Figures 159 and 160).

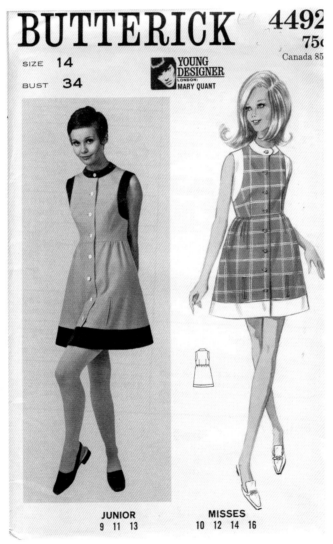

FIGURE 159 *Mary Quant One-Piece Dress. Butterick 4492, 1967.579.URI. Butterick B4492. Image courtesy of the McCall Pattern Company, copyright 2013.*

FIGURE 160 *Rudi Gernreich Misses' Dress. New York Designers' Collection Plus, McCall 1011, 1967.395.URI. McCall's M1101. Image courtesy of the McCall Pattern Company, copyright 2013.*

Advertising budgets were increased, and celebrity spokespeople from film and TV were recruited to promote the patterns. Two popular TV stars, Marie Osmond and Marlo Thomas, teamed up with Butterick and McCall respectively. The companies also actively recruited African American designers and models. For example, Willi Smith designed patterns for Butterick and McCall. The expansion included African-inspired designs including the fashionable dashiki (see Figure 161).

FIGURE 161 *The Dashiki. Men's shirt in two lengths or misses' dress in two lengths. Simplicity 5043, 1975.157.URI. Commercial Pattern Archive.*

Miniskirts and short shorts led to the increased popularity of skintight bodysuits, tights, and leotards. Originally worn by dancers, these garments were adopted first by the "bohemian" movement and then migrated into mainstream fashions. Thanks to the introduction of stretch fabrics and the new "reverse cycle" sewing machines for stitching those fabrics, pattern companies joined the bandwagon and offered patterns for all of these stretch garments (see Figure 162).

FIGURE 162 *Misses' Bodysuit. Vogue 8441, 1972.367.URI. Vogue V8441. Image courtesy of the McCall Pattern Company, copyright 2013.*

Established Companies

By the mid-1960s, there were four major pattern manufacturers: Butterick/Vogue, McCall, Simplicity in the United States, and Associated British Patterns in Britain. Advance Pattern Company stopped producing patterns around 1965. Syndicated companies producing patterns included Spadea, which continued until around 1976, Famous Features until 1996, and Reader Mail until 2008.

The German publishing company Burda had introduced *Burda Moden* (*Burda Fashion*) in 1950 and began including pattern supplement sheets, similar to the *Harper's Bazar* overlay pattern sheets of the nineteenth century, in 1952. The sheets contained several patterns, the shapes of which were defined with coded, colored dashes, dots, asterisks, and so forth. These were internationally popular and began to have an impact on the American and British markets by the 1960s. The patterns sheets occasionally included two sizes of a pattern, but usually only one size was provided. The company's success and influence persists to the present with patterns distributed in envelopes as well as overlay pattern sheets. Early patterns were often considered difficult to work with since they did not include a seam allowance (see Figures 163 and 164).

Mergers

In April 1961, Butterick bought and licensed the name and trademark of the Vogue patterns and pattern publications (but not *Vogue* magazine) in the expectation of substantially enlarging its share of the market. The two brands were complementary; Butterick patterns were essentially

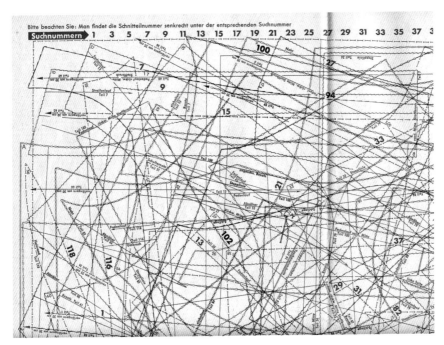

FIGURE 163 *Burda Overlay Supplement Pattern Sheet. Includes 7026 (partial sheet).* Burda Moden, *January 1968. Includes separate "English Supplement" with descriptions and pattern piece diagrams. Commercial Pattern Archive.*

for the mass market with a price range of $0.40 to $0.75 (equivalent to $5.35 in 2011), and Vogue patterns were considered to be high style with a price range of $0.75 to $3.50. The latter were couturier patterns complete with a cloth label to be sewn into the complete garment (see Figure 165). Kathleen McDermott compiled an unpublished in-house history entitled "From 'Old Lady' to Industry Leader: Butterick, 1960–1992," tracing the ownerships of the company. She observed that the expectation was successful enough to attract the acquisition of Butterick/Vogue by American Can, "among the largest printers in the world," in 1968 (McDermott 1993: 10). That same year McCall combined with Canada Dry and Hunt-Wesson Food as part of the Norton-Simon, Inc. conglomerate (Dickson 1979: 167).

New Companies

Several new independent pattern enterprises were formed between 1967 and 1979. In response to the increased availability and use of stretch fabrics, Kerstin Martensson founded Sew-Knit-N-Stretch, Inc. and designed patterns with that brand name as well as Kwik Sew. For both, she designed patterns for lingerie, swimwear, active wear, and polar fleece (see Figure 166). Ann Person started Stretch & Sew Pattern Company in 1967. Their patterns were multi-sized for a wide range of sizes. Originally for knits only, the patterns expanded for other kinds of fabrics by 1993.[1]

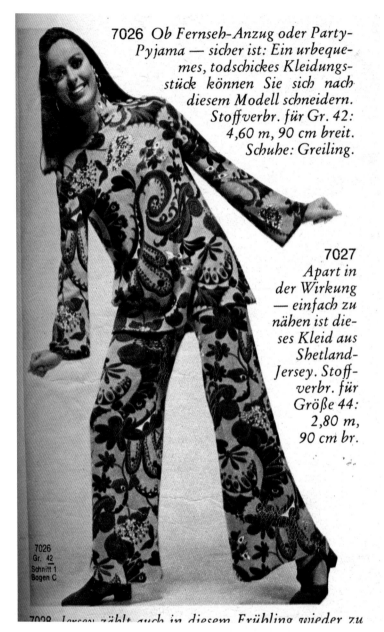

7026 *Ob Fernseh-Anzug oder Party-Pyjama — sicher ist: Ein urbequemes, todschickes Kleidungsstück können Sie sich nach diesem Modell schneidern. Stoffverbr. für Gr. 42: 4,60 m, 90 cm breit. Schuhe: Greiling.*

7027 *Apart in der Wirkung — einfach zu nähen ist dieses Kleid aus Shetland-Jersey. Stoffverbr. für Größe 44: 2,80 m, 90 cm br.*

7026
Gr. 42
Schnitt 1
Bogen C

7028 *Iersey zählt auch in diesem Frühling wieder zu*

FIGURE 164 *Smart Trouser Suit. 7206, 7207, Burda Moden, January 1968. Commercial Pattern Archive.*

FIGURE 165 *One-Piece Dress. Vogue 1135, Couturier designed by John Cavanagh of England, 1962.246.URI. Vogue V1135. Image courtesy of the McCall Pattern Company, copyright 2013.*

Folkwear, the most influential new pattern company of the 1970s, was founded by three women with a "passion for finely crafted ethnic clothing." Originally owned by Kate Mathews, pattern designer Lisa Sanders, and illustrator Gretchen Schields, the company was sold to Taunton Press in the mid-1980s and then to Lark Books before going back to the original group in 2002. The company continues to offer a variety of ethnic and historic patterns as well as patterns for accessories. The patterns are not designed with the latest fashion in mind, so many are reissued

FIGURE 166 *Ladies' One-Piece Swimsuit. Kwik Sew 150, 1968.751.URI. Kwik Sew K0150. Image courtesy of the McCall Pattern Company, copyright 2013.*

over several years.[2] The patterns are multi-size, and the ethnic patterns usually combine women's and men's sizes in one package. Many contain information details on the origins and uses of the garments as well as needlework instructions as needed (see Figure 167).

Two examples of a variety of independent companies included Daisy Kingdom,[3] founded in the late 1960s, and Green Pepper, established in 1973. They specialized in outdoor sportswear patterns that were sold as part of a kit, which included all the fabrics and notions to complete the

FIGURE 167 *Egyptian Shirt and Appliqué Design. Folkwear 104, 1976.509.URI. Illustration by Gretchen Schields, with permission of Folkwear Patterns.*

garment. Both companies were located in Oregon. These independent companies identified special markets, making patterns for specialized fabrics and specific needs and interests. Most were established by women working out of their homes and locating their firms in smaller urban areas around the United States.

Summary

The 1960s and 1970s can be defined as a revolt against tradition, and this is certainly expressed in the fashions of the era. The tensions of the revolt were expressed in the conflict between natural and synthetic fibers, sedate colors influenced by natural dyes versus bright psychedelic colors from newly developed synthetic dyes, and defiant fashions for both women and men. In responses not dissimilar to the impulses that inspired the aesthetic movement at the height of the Industrial Revolution, there was a revival of interest in nature and shunning of mass-manufactured items. The pattern companies were quick to support the newly inspired styles as well as the traditional with emphasis on the value of individually crafted garments. They sought to elevate pattern sales with aggressive promotion thorough expanded advertising in all media as well as strong associations with various celebrities. Simultaneously, they were responsive to newly developed synthetic, easy-care fabrics and stretch fabrics. They promoted the changing fashions while working to promote the options for individuality, which was a pillar of the boom period for pattern sales in the 1960s.

The established companies continued to dominate the market, although new niche-market pattern companies such as Folkwear, Kwik Sew, and Sew-Knit-N-Stretch were gaining popularity. Syndicated pattern companies such as Reader Mail and Famous Features continued to fill the needs of the conventional market. The international expansion of the major companies and the outreach of the German company Burda reached a broader global market. In response to continued complaints about the fit of the patterns, new sizing standards were introduced in 1967 to relate more directly to ready-to-wear sizes and to better fit the altered proportions of the consumers.

The pattern companies were meeting the challenges, but more were on the horizon. New technology with increased computerization, the shift to two-member working families, changing attitudes, and the emergence of the movement introduced in 1975 with John Molloy's *Dress for Success* books influenced points of view of the 1980s.

12

Reinvention and Renaissance

1980s–2010

The 1980s and 1990s are characterized as the age of conspicuous consumption. However, six other identifiable stylistic influences were present. These included the dress for success movement, the "preppy" look, the ragtag look, romanticism, historicism, and the physical fitness initiative.

John Molloy's (1975, 1977) *Dress for Success* books became the bibles for young, ambitious personnel, stressing neatness and clean lines with precise formulas for selecting appropriate clothing for the workplace. The archetypal business look for women became "power suits" with

FIGURE 168 *Misses' Jackets. Simplicity 1462, 1934.2.URI. Commercial Pattern Archive. Adrian-inspired sleeves. Misses' jacket made from Simplicity 1462 by Roberta Hale, with permission from Roberta Hale.*

FIGURE 169 *Misses' Blouse and Skirt. Vogue 2185, 1988.44.URI. Image courtesy of the McCall Pattern Company, copyright 2013.*

FIGURE 170 *Misses' Dress. Butterick 3014, 1988.50.URI. Butterick B3014. Image courtesy of the McCall Pattern Company, copyright 2013.*

FIGURE 171 *Sets of Shoulder Pads and Couture Shoulder Pads. Sets of shoulder pads, Butterick 3276, 1945.35.BWS. Couture shoulder pads, Vogue 8817, 1983.460.URI. Butterick 3276. Image courtesy of the McCall Pattern Company, copyright 2013. Vogue 8817. Image courtesy of the McCall Pattern Company, copyright 2013.*

padded shoulders and wide lapels. The 1950s "preppy" look, revived in the 1980s, served as casual dress. Both were in sharp contrast to the extended ragtag styles of the "punk" look, which continued into the 1990s. In contrast to the power-suit mentality, romantic modes were rekindled, partially inspired by the courtship and wedding of Charles, Prince of Wales, and Princess Diana in 1981 (see Figures 168 and 169). Romanticism was expressed with echoes of 1930s fashions with large or full puffed sleeves, as well as influences from the 1940s with bustles and shoulder pads (see Figures 170 and 171). In the 1990s, historicism was fueled by nostalgia. Rekindled interest in patterns from previous decades prompted pattern companies to reissue earlier styles as Vintage (Vogue and Simplicity) and Retro (Butterick), and the growing number of reenactors' needs for suitable historical garments prompted designs for patterns from a range of historical eras. Additional eclecticism included the strong interest in physical fitness, jogging, and workouts that required specially designed garments (see Figure 172).

FIGURE 172 *Misses', Men's, or Teen Boys' Tops, Cardigan, Pants, Shorts, and Multicolor Transfer. Tops and cardigan for stretch only. McCall 4386, 1988.166.URI. McCall's M4386. Image courtesy of the McCall Pattern Company, copyright 2013.*

New Technology

The 1980s witnessed a burst of computer technological. The technology was incorporated in pattern companies' business practices in manufacturing and marketing procedures. By 1991, when restricted commercial use of the Internet was lifted, pattern companies embraced it to rapidly market their designs. Companies began to use computer applications to trim costs, to improve

FIGURE 173 *Misses' Dress or Top, Skirt, and Scarf. Focus on sergers/overlock. Mc-Call 3264, 1987.225.URI. McCall's M3264. Image courtesy of the McCall Pattern Company, copyright 2013.*

inventory control, and to boost productivity. For example, Simplicity used an application to streamline procedures for processing discarded patterns. An information sheet released by Microsystems Technology stated the original process took several weeks four times a year; the computer application cut time in one processing step from fifteen minutes to forty-five seconds and the company reduced the staff from twenty-eight to four, thereby "ushering in a new era of efficiency in internal operations" (n.d.: n.p.). Furthermore, computer-aided design (CAD) applications for personal computers allowed individuals to design new patterns and print them for publication. This led to an explosion of independent pattern enterprises.

In addition, sewing machine manufacturers began making computer-controlled machines. For example, Singer's "Touchtronic" sewing machine was introduced in 1978 and by 1990 incorporated the largest microprocessor in a machine. The model 9900 included an LED message center offering practical advice to the sewer. Another machine available to the home sewer by 1990 was a serger or overlock;[1] it was ideal for working with popular single- or double-knit fabrics. Pattern companies quickly recognized an opportunity and created numerous patterns with special instructions for sewing with a serger (see Figure 173).

Existing Companies

Pattern companies were struggling by the 1980s. The ranks of working mothers increased dramatically and pattern sales began to slump, as did related home sewing goods such as fabrics and notions. Many independent fabric stores were forced to close. All the existing companies began to place greater emphasis on crafts such as quilting and Halloween costumes since these were proving to be the most popular. They established strong relationships with chain fabric stores such as So-Fro and Jo-Ann Fabrics, which were emphasizing crafts as creative hobbies for the working women.

The last decades of the twentieth century were marked with mergers and buyouts. Butterick and Vogue were considered a single company with two brands. In 1983, Butterick's management purchased the company from American Can, assuming a high level of debt. To reduce costs, Butterick reduced staff and inventory and eliminated all its printing and distribution plants except for the main one in Altoona, Pennsylvania. In the article "Reaping from Sewing" in *Forbes* magazine, Jean Chatzky observed that the company invested in computerized design systems, which speeded up the time it took to get a new pattern to market. The new machines

cut the time it takes for getting a new pattern to market from 2½ months to as little as 4 weeks. Speed-to-market is important because pattern designs are typically knocked off from popular styles or licensed from hot designers like Donna Ban [*sic*] and Ralph Lauren. Unless the patternmaker is quick, a dress can be on the remainder rack before its pattern is available in stores. (Chatzky 1992: 154)

The author may be referring to Donna Karan, who designed for Vogue Patterns and also designed for Ray-Ban eyeglasses in the 1990s. In addition, Butterick Patterns nearly doubled the total number of less expensive patterns between 1988 and early 1992. The "See & Sew" line was introduced in 1977 for $0.99. The patterns were popular since they were less complicated than regular Butterick patterns and easy to make. By 1981, the price was $1.19 (equivalent to $2.69 in 2011) compared to the $2.75 pattern average (equivalent to $6.69 in 2011).

The major companies expanded their crafts and accessories pattern series to include home furnishings, children's costumes, stuffed toys, and a variety of accessories. In keeping with the "designer pattern company" image, Vogue added the Individualist in 1983, Career in 1989, and Attitudes International in 1991 to the Paris Original and American Designer pattern series. Prices for these increased from a top price of $10.00 (equivalent to $21.00 in 2011) in the mid-1980s to $17.50 in 1990 and $25.00 (equivalent to $33.40 in 2011) in 1998. Vogue introduced Vintage Vogue in 1998 at the top price. The initial selections were from 1940s Vogue patterns (see Figure 174). The pattern was

FIGURE 174 *Misses' Jacket, Dress, and Belt. Vintage Vogue 2196, 1998.18.URI. Vogue V2196. Image courtesy of the McCall Pattern Company, copyright 2013.*

graded to conform to 1990s measurements, and the instruction sheets were revised to match those of present-day Vogue patterns. Butterick issued Retro Butterick in 1999, but fewer patterns were issued and the series was less expensive than Vogue's. To facilitate and encourage home sewing, Vogue subscribed to the practice of including sewing skill ratings of very easy, easy, average, and advanced on some patterns. The Today's Fit series by Sandra Betzina, founder of the Power Sewing books, TV shows, and online sewing classes, was added in 1999 (see Figure 175).

FIGURE 175 *Misses'/Misses' Petite Jacket. Vogue 7334, 2001.34.URI. Today's Fit by Sandra Betzina. Vogue V7334. Image courtesy of the McCall Pattern Company, copyright 2013.*

McCall also struggled with women's shift away from home sewing. To promote the ease of sewing, McCall initiated "Show-Me," a visual sewing system for the new or unsure sewer, in the late 1970s. It consisted of a three-booklet starter set purchased with any "Show-Me" pattern. They formed an alliance with Pati Palmer and Susan Pletsch, the first licensees for a pattern company who were not ready-to-wear designers, movie stars, or TV stars. They were established authors of sewing manuals and created the eight-hour blazer, which became an industry best

FIGURE 176 *Misses' Dress and Petticoat. By Shari Belafonte-Harper. McCall 3300, 1987.237.URI. McCall's M3300. Image courtesy of the McCall Pattern Company, copyright 2013.*

seller in 1980. The partnership with TV star Marlo Thomas in the 1970s was very successful and was continued with new affiliations with rising celebrities. Brooke Shields, a child and teen model and *Vogue* cover girl, was to appeal to the youthful customer. Shari Belafonte-Harper, film and TV actress, model, and singer, was to appeal to twenty- and thirtysomethings and African Americans (see Figure 176). Costume designer Nolan Miller and *Dynasty*'s stars promoted the extremes of conspicuous consumption for the slightly more mature and sophisticated (see Figure 177).

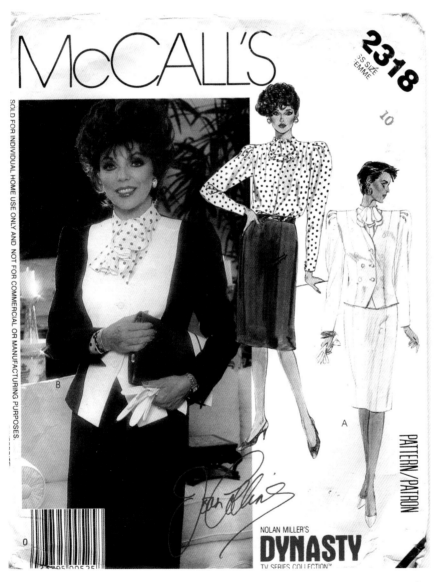

FIGURE 177 *Misses' Jacket, Blouse, and Skirt. McCall 2318, 1986.14.URI. Nolan Miller's Dynasty Collection; Joan Collins. McCall's M2318. Image courtesy of the McCall Pattern Company, copyright 2013.*

In spite of all these initiatives, McCall experienced difficulties. It was bought and sold twice between 1983 and 1987 before filing for Chapter 11 bankruptcy in 1988. After various negotiations, McCall emerged from bankruptcy and concentrated on revitalizing and adjusting to the needs of the future customer, promoting sewing for gratification and making craft items. To that end, the company had launched profitable campaigns, which included patterns for overlock stitching and printed pattern for knitting machines. The company continued to promote "Easy" patterns and "Stitch 'N Save" in 1982 to compete with Butterick's "See & Sew." Others included the Woman's Day collection, Nancy Zieman's Busy Woman's and Creative Woman's sewing patterns, and fifty- and ninety-minute patterns, which really meant sewing time not cutting and sewing. By 1988, the company phased out the practice of printing three or more sizes in one pattern begun in the mid-1960s. Multi-sized patterns required basic shapes, which limited design features; single-sized patterns allowed for more details for a more elegant garment.

All the major companies had licensed fashion affiliates with designers, personalities, and retail labels. According to Peggy Bendel (1987b), reporter for *Sew News* in October 1987, McCall's topped the list, with twenty-five names showing the variety, including French Connection, Jones of New York, Liz Claiborne, Looney Tunes, Raggedy Ann and Andy, and Wizard of Oz.

Although Simplicity had the largest share of the pattern market in the 1970s, it was not immune to the downturn of home sewing in the 1980s. *Women's Wear Daily* reported Simplicity's sales slumped from $112 million in 1975 to $65 million in 1984 (Rutberg 1993: 12). However, the popularity of their patterns appealed to a broad strata of society as implied by the first "Moonie" mass wedding, in 1982, in New York's Madison Square Garden, when 2,075 couples were married.[2] Each bride's wedding gown was made from Simplicity pattern 8392 (see Figure 178).

The company changed hands four times before being bought by Conso International Co. in 1998. The acquisition complemented Conso's merchandise, which included decorative trimmings, and was further expanded with the acquisition of ribbon and trim maker Wm. E. Wright in 2000. During the 1980s and 1990s, Simplicity employed marketing tactics similar to those of the other companies. They diversified their pattern styles, drawing in new affiliations with personalities such as Christie Brinkley and designers including Alfred Sung and Carol Horn of New Directions. The children's pattern lines were expanded to include Gunne Sax and Cinderella. Along with the other companies, they created a line of patterns specifically for sergers. The accessories and crafts lines were expanded with licenses with Walt Disney, among others, for stuffed toys and costumes. Simplicity became the lead producer of quality period patterns for reenactors, from medieval to Civil War–era patterns by designers Andrea Schewe and Martha McCain (see Figure 179).

Simplicity acquired three additional pattern companies, each with its own brand name. Style, the number-one pattern brand in the United Kingdom, was bought in 1986. Simplicity's president, Richard Gyde, labeled Style patterns as "upscale, like Lord & Taylor, and Simplicity patterns, like Spiegel" (Bendel 1987a: 42). The market identified for Style patterns was career-oriented women with an interest in the latest contemporary fashions. Seven top British designers were under contract: Zandra Rhodes, Bruce Oldfield, Rifat Ozbek, Murray Arbeid, Jasper Conran, Margaret Howell, and Janice Wainwright. Simplicity also acquired New Look, another British company, in 1987. Founded in the late 1920s as Maudella Patterns, the company changed its name to the English Pattern Company and then was rechristened New Look to highlight a focus on trendy fashions. The designers were ready-to-wear designers rather than fashion names.

FIGURE 178 *Misses' Bridal or Bridesmaids' Dress. Simplicity 8392, Simplicity Counter Catalog, March 1978: 895. Commercial Pattern Archive. Chosen for the 1982 mass Moonie wedding.*

The third purchase in 1987 was Reader Mail, the syndicated pattern–producing group, allowing Simplicity to cover a full range of pattern needs, from the most basic styles (syndicated patterns) to classic styles (Simplicity patterns) to trendy high fashion with Style and New Look patterns. Prior to the acquisition of Reader Mail and New Look, Simplicity had followed the trend set by the other major companies and introduced Extra-Sure Pattern (E.S.P.) for $1.25 in 1981 and a "Super Saver" pattern line selling for $1.99 in 1986. Their regular patterns were averaging $2.50–$3.50 in 1981. They promoted "Overnight Success" and "Fuss-Free-Fit" along with other promotional

FIGURE 179 *Medieval Gown. Simplicity 8725 designed by Martha McCain*, Simplicity Counter Catalog, *Autumn 2000, with permission of Martha Kelly (Martha McCain).*

tactics to encourage the novice sewer as well as active support for the American Home Sewing Association's campaign to change sewing's image to draw in more beginners.

Rosaline Lemontree (1983) wrote an evaluation of the pattern companies' application of the term "easy" in *Sew News* August/September. She pointed out that the companies' original accepted criteria was five or fewer main pattern pieces with no tricky details such as clipping into corners and a clear, simple instruction sheet. However, the distinctions became blurred as more names were coined by the companies. Simplicity's Jiffy, Super Jiffy, Beginner's Choice, and Overnight Success implied all were easy to sew. This was not always true. McCall's Easy and Make It Tonight may have had more than five pieces, but the construction was easy and the guide sheets were "the best in the business" (Lemontree 1983: 33). Butterick's Fast and Easy, Yes! It's Easy!, and Timeless Fashions estimated two to four hours to make them. Very Easy Vogue required a higher level of sewing skills because they included a variety of design elements, such as more than five pieces and top stitching. In 1986, Butterick/Vogue introduced beginner, average, and advanced sewing rating on some patterns. Vogue Ultra Ez, a less expensive line selling for $6.95 compared to the average Vogue pattern price of $10.95, began in 1992.

Independent Pattern Enterprises

Independent companies defined categories of specialization and did limited pattern production. They are "the ones to go to for specialized fit, style or construction methods that go beyond the standard sewing pattern boundaries" (Miller 2012: 66). Further, the designs are not subject to rapid fashion changes. Companies such as Babe Too!, Elizabeth Lee Designs, Raindrops and Roses, and Patch Couturier specialize in maternity clothing adaptable for nursing mothers, baby carriers, and decorations for a nursery. Others such as Children's Corner, Enchanted Panda, Penny and Co., and Belles and Beaus specialize in patterns for infants, toddlers, and young children, some with instructions for heirloom sewing techniques and smocking patterns.

Interest in wearable art inspired several new companies, often associated with quilting, that applied the same techniques to detailing vests patterns. Others, such as Bristles and Needles, supplied stencils for hand-painting fabrics to be made into garments from the included pattern. Lois Ericson, an established fiber artist, created a pattern line, Design & Sew. Ericson retired in 2009 (see Figure 180). A variation on the approach to wearable art is practiced by the Sewing Workshop, a sewing and arts school with a small notions department and a sister pattern line, the Sewing Workshop Collection, designed by participants in the workshop. In addition to the patterns, the company offers classes and workshops regularly (see Figure 181).

Companies devoted to equestrian, Western wear, and folk or square dance clothing included Jean Hardy Pattern Co., Authentic Patterns, and Square D Fashions. Square D acquired Authentic at some point and closed in 2011; Jean Hardy continues with an online catalog of patterns. An additional group of small companies provides service to reenactors and other individuals looking to make period garments. These include Medieval Miscellanea and Past Patterns. Sandra Altman, owner and founder of Past Patterns, makes historical clothing patterns based on authentic garments and vintage patterns. The date range for her patterns is the 1780s to the 1940s. Other companies specializing in vintage pattern reproduction include Decades of Style and Eva Dress.

All this activity from independent pattern companies did not mean the mainstream companies were ignoring the market the small companies were servicing. Each company carried children's clothing and was involved in high-profile arrangements with major popular brands such as Disney, Looney Tunes, and other popular film franchises to make children's costumes. Adult costume lines were expanded to include well-researched period patterns.

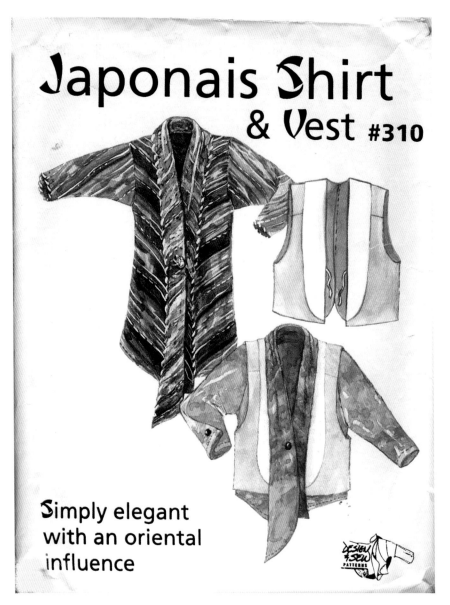

FIGURE 180 *Japonais Shirt and Vest. Design & Sew 310, 1995.92.URI. Designed by Lois Ericson and Diane Ericson. Courtesy of Diane Ericson.*

German Pattern Companies

Burda, the German pattern company, was distributing patterns in twenty countries around the world by 1987. The company's marketing strategies included "super-easy," "start," "intermediate," and "regular" sewing skills designations along with Burda Couture, Studio, and Super Combination lines. Further, they promoted the idea of not including seam allowances in their patterns,

FIGURE 181 *Lotus Skirt. The Sewing Workshop, 2008.23.URI, with permission of Linda Lee, Sewing Workshop. Estimated Date.*

leaving that task to the cutter/sewer to give a better fit to the finished garment. At some point in the late 1990s, Burda included seams and hems.

A second German company, Neue Mode–USA, was gaining a small presence with pattern retailers and on the Internet. Neue Mode offers less expensive patterns; the average cost is $4.95. The average of companies' prices ranges from $10.00–$25.00. Like Burda, they initially offered overlay pattern sheets as supplements in *Neue Mode* magazine; they added individual patterns in envelopes in the 1990s. The patterns are multi-sized, and seam allowances need to be added.

New Millennium

Additional realignment occurred with the new millennium. In spite of a resurgence of interest in home sewing marked by the formation of national sewing associations and guilds, the major pattern companies needed to continue to downsize. Once again, a merger was deemed necessary. McCall acquired Butterick/Vogue in 2001. The new conglomerate hallmarked each brand: Butterick is designated as "Classical," McCall as "Contemporary," and Vogue "Couture."

McCall, Butterick, Vogue, Simplicity, and New Look continued into the twenty-first century. Simplicity discontinued Style in 2000. Burda and Neue Mode held a small percentage of the market in the United States. Independent companies that expanded beyond their original specializations include Kwik Sew (acquired by McCall in 2011) and Folkwear. Kwik Sew Europe, a distributor of Kwik Sew patterns in the Scandinavian countries since 1989, added the United Kingdom in 2004 and the rest of Europe in 2005.

Independent companies flourished and the number increased dramatically. A few went out of business when the owner/founder retired, but others took up the challenge. A search of the Internet for independent pattern companies will provide a wide sampling, but not a comprehensive list, of active companies. Patterns are sold through mail order via the Internet or through retail chains such as Walmart or Jo-Ann Fabrics. In addition, several companies have created an online community utilizing online tech-craft. Patterns are available for downloading and printing on home printers for a fee. It is instant gratification, no waiting for the post to deliver traditional patterns purchased from online catalogs or buying them from a retail outlet. Companies such as Fitz Patterns only offer downloadable sewing patterns, while others such as Sewing Workshop and La Fred offer patterns by mail or download. Burda joined the online community in 2007. By 2011, McCall was offering a few patterns through their online catalog; the other U.S. brands were not. However, auxiliary enterprises, such as www.sewingpatterns.com, have online pattern stores offering a wide range of downloadable patterns, including some of the major brands.

The made-to-measure pattern idea was resurrected with companies such as Fit Me Patterns, formerly Unique Custom Pattern Company. The company maintains a web catalog. With the advent of computer-aided pattern drafting software, patterns can be drafted to a customer's individual measurements following directions in the company's booklet or the CD instructional kit. Lekco patterns sell CDs with special CAD software that will generate a custom fitted pattern when the user inputs four measurements. The pattern can be printed on a desktop printer.

Summary

Aggressive promotions, with traditional pattern companies vying for strong positions in a shifting marketplace, occurred throughout the 1980s and 1990s. When the buyouts and mergers were settled in 2011, there were two remaining major traditional companies, McCall and Simplicity, with five brand names: McCall, Butterick, Vogue, Simplicity, and New Look. Alan Clandenning (2001) of the *Times Union, Albany* noted that the five brand names commanded about 72 to 75 percent of the market according to the Federal Trade Commission. For the established smaller companies, New Look merged with Simplicity and Kwik Sew merged with McCall; Folkwear is independent and, along with the other independent companies, have a small percentage of pattern sales. Kwik Sew Europe experienced international expansion, and the German companies Burda and Neue Mode developed a broader presence in North America and gained a small percentage of pattern sales.

Simultaneously, independent companies were carving out niche markets. The increasing number of these companies belied the sense that "no one was sewing anymore." Major factors that

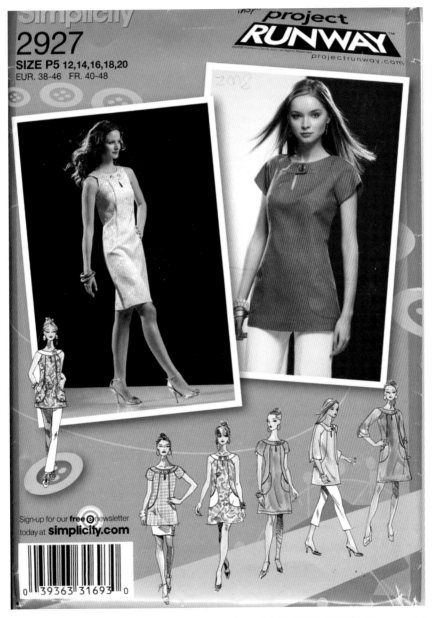

FIGURE 182 *Misses' Dress or Tunic. Simplicity 2927, 2008.46.URI. Commercial Pattern Archive. Inspired by* Project Runway.

enabled these companies to flourish were the explosion of computer technology, computer-aided design software, the growth of the Internet, and personal computers, as well as individual sewers' ability to download and print patterns for immediate use.

Advances in sewing machine technology stimulated interest in sewing. On May 20, 2011, the *Wall Street Journal* reported "amid sewing's pop-culture revival, makers of sewing machines are cutting no corners in their appeal to the next generation of seamstresses" (Athavaley 2011: D1). The new sewing machines are equipped with USB ports, automatic threading, decorative stitches, and high-resolution screens, which allows for multitasking. There are smartphone apps to assist with matching thread to fabric as well as software that digitizes embroidery designs. Athavaley credits the influence of *Project Runway*[3] for sewing's "pop-culture revival" (see Figure 182)." Renewed interest expanded sewing machine production and increased the need for fabric and notions outlets. Walmart removed fabric departments in 2006 only to bring them back to meet demand.

The greatest changes in the 150-plus years of commercial pattern production are the clothing styles, and even those are resurrected and reinterpreted regularly. The pattern-making process is essentially the same as the earliest days from design to model to the pattern master for reproduction. The tools and production aids have been modernized and upgraded regularly in efforts to streamline production to be at the forefront of the latest fashion trends. Two of the original pioneers of the industry, Butterick and McCall, have a predominant presence. Though incorporated somewhat later, Simplicity has maintained its strength, and numerous original nineteenth-century pattern companies have been replaced with equally numerous small, independent companies in the last forty years. The practice of home sewing ceased to be a necessity in every home and has become a "hobby." The pleasure of making one's garments or decorative soft goods persisted and gained popularity. Sewing associations have stimulated interest and revived home sewing for satisfaction and sense of accomplishment.

Epilogue

The advent of the U.S. commercial pattern industry in the late 1850s was a coalition of numerous factors: experimentation with more and economical methods for fulfilling clothing needs for everyone, technological advances with sewing machines, wood-based paper and textile production, and improved communication of the latest fashions inspired by the nineteenth-century entrepreneurial spirit. Founders of the pattern companies responded to the prevailing climate and capitalized on the new developments for making clothing for all. In general, the companies included a publishing component to promote clothing patterns. The founders explored a variety of pattern-making techniques, including complex pattern drafting systems, small diagrams, single-size overlapping pattern sheets, and full-size tissue paper patterns. The latter ultimately dominated the market and are still in use today.

What has changed? Economic shifts throughout the twentieth century led to mergers and incorporations, shifting family-owned businesses with a major single product to corporations that are umbrellas for several products. The shift appeared to bring minor changes, but each pattern company/brand name was competing for predominance within the corporation as well as in the marketplace. Still two of the original nineteenth-century companies, Butterick and McCall, and two from the early twentieth century, Vogue and Simplicity, have survived and prospered while others were bought out or simply failed. Some, such as DuBarry, were affiliated with chain stores that went out of business. Others, such as Hollywood, fulfilled the original purpose of an inexpensive counterbalance for Vogue patterns during the Great Depression and were dropped.

The needs of the market underwent significant changes. Clothing manufacture moved from the homemaker and dressmaker to mass production. In addition, women who had primarily been limited to the home entered the workforce outside the home and had less time to pursue sewing interests. Sewing shifted from being a necessary skill to one of creative expression and an interesting hobby. The pattern companies adapted their product to supply those interests. Crafts pattern lines were expanded, vintage or "retro" patterns resized to the current sizing criteria, and period "costume" lines designed for reenactors were introduced.

Simultaneously, new niche market pattern companies formed. They followed the footsteps of the original companies as family-owned companies. However, they did not follow current fashion trends. Instead they concentrated on timeless fashions and patterns designed for specific markets, utilizing the latest computer-based technology to capture a percentage, albeit small, of the market. These companies are numerous and located throughout North America and have a strong presence on the Internet.

Finally, the history of pattern companies must be viewed in conjunction with all the home sewing–related enterprises. From the outset, the sewing machine was a major enabler and continues to be so. Sergers or overlock machines for domestic use and computerized sewing machines have stimulated pattern usage. The decline of independent fabric stores has had a depressing effect on the market, but there is some evidence that a demand for fabrics will stimulate a revival in retail outlets. For example, in my small community there are now two retail shops specializing in fabrics and supplies for home sewers and quilters. Each shop offers classes to encourage more sewing activity.

It remains to be seen what effect the current global economic crisis will have on home sewing. However, in my vicinity, sewing master classes are attracting women of all ages; sewing associations such as the Association of Sewing Professionals and the Center for Pattern Design are energetic and productive. The online activity of the pattern companies and the burgeoning number of independent companies does make clear that there is the persistent desire for patterns, the essential tools for creating garments whether for a special individual or a special occasion. The proclamation made by *The Designer* in 1916 still holds true: that the paper dress pattern is "Truly one of the great elemental inventions in the world's history—The Tissue of Dreams."

Appendix

Pattern Grids Rendered
by Susan Hannel

The patterns included are samples of fashionable styles from 1850 to the 1960s. All the selected patterns are cut and punched; they are not duplicates but are created in the style of the originals and have been further altered to conform to present-day pattern practices. The pattern pieces are laid out to show the straight-of-grain, and 0.5-inch seam allowances are marked. Each grid is a prototype tracing the development of cut and punched pattern production during these years. By the mid-1960s, the major pattern companies abandoned cut and punched patterns in favor of printed patterns first introduced by McCall's in 1921.

For example, the presentation of the Demorest basque pattern is typical of early patterns. The pieces of the original pattern are not identified on the sheet; the side panel is upside down and the half sleeve is sideways at the bottom of the sheet to work within the space on the paper. The cap of the sleeve is identified as "N:4."

The Domestic pattern for the misses' dress represents standard cut and punched patterns for the late nineteenth century. The original pieces are marked with notches and a series of small perforations. In this specific instance, the seamstress is expected to identify each piece by the shape and join them to make the finished dress. There is a list of the pieces in the pattern such as "upper and under front," the latter identified on the pattern grid as the lining. The brief instructions direct the seamstress to cut the collar on a "crosswise thread" and the skirt on the cross grain. The rest of the instructions detail the sequence for sewing the dress together.

The patterns for the shirtwaist and seven-gored skirt, typical of the predominant silhouette of 1912, are also cut and punched although there is greater variety on the perforations to include crosses, large and small holes, and notches. The patterns also include pieces such as facings and plackets. The envelope includes a construction chart showing how to piece the garments together. The 1929 Vogue pattern includes a diagram of the pattern pieces on the envelope to aid the seamstress in identifying the various pieces and their orientation on the grain of the fabric. In addition, each piece is identified with a letter punched out in a series of small holes and the girdle is in green tissue rather than tan. "All seams are allowed" but not marked in the pattern.

The other four patterns—Simplicity's 1937 blouse and 1942 coverall, Advance dress, and Spadea Nehru jacket—all include well-illustrated and detailed instructions sheets. Unmarked seam allowance is identified on each sheet. All except Spadea conform to measurements recommended by the Bureau of Standards of the U.S. Department of Commerce. Spadea's jacket sizing followed ready-to-wear body measurements.

Basque 1854

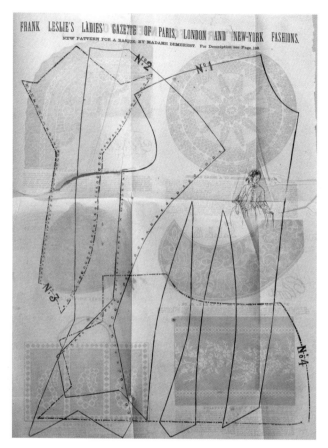

FIGURE 183 *Demorest Basque. 1854.1.URI.* Frank Leslie's Ladies' Gazette of Paris, London and New York Fashions. *Pattern sheet supplement; bust thirty-eight inches. Courtesy of the Kent State University Museum.*

Four pieces: basque front, side-body, back, sleeve. Separate facings of sufficient width for the bottom of the basque and sleeve need to be cut. Match notches to close seams.

1 Stitch front fitting darts.

2 Join side-body to fronts and back.

3 Join the center back.

4 Face the bottom edge.

5 Cut bias strip 2 inches wide by 17 inches long for neck binding and bind the neck.

6 Stitch underarm seam.

7 Set in sleeve with seam along front of arm.

8 Work buttonholes and stitch on buttons.

9 Finish trimmings.

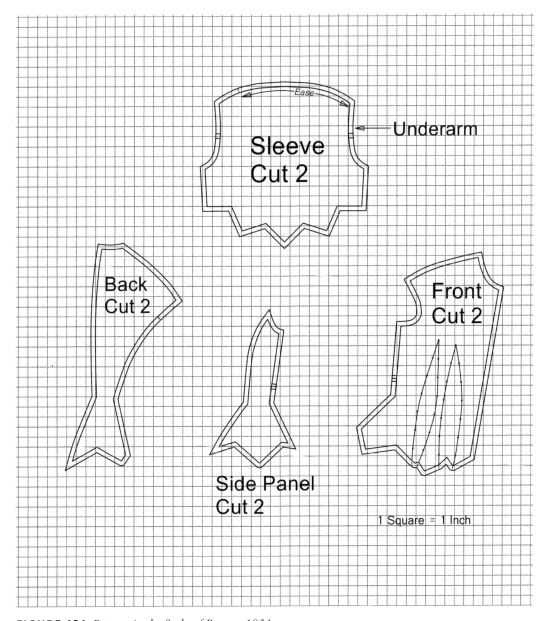

FIGURE 184 *Pattern in the Style of Basque 1854.*

Misses' Domestic Dress 1890

FIGURE 185 *Misses' Dress. Domestic 4575, 1890.5.URI. Commercial Pattern Archive.*

Thirteen years, bust 30 inches, requires 8 yards of 21-inch or 4 yards of 42-inch goods; if plaid trimming, 1 yard of 42-inch goods, ⅜ yards piqué for vest, and ¼ yards lace trimming, or one piece ribbon velvet and 4½ yards of wider ribbon velvet.

Eight pieces: lining front and back, upper-front, upper-back, side-body, sleeve, collar, and half skirt.

Match notches to close seams: 1-inch seam allowance on shoulder and underarm seams, ⅜-inch on all others.

1   Stitch front darts of lining.

2   Turn the hem on front edge of upper-front as notched, make two pleats toward center front and place on lining.

3 Make three tucks toward center back in upper-back by meeting every two notches and place on the lining, turning the hems together.

4 Close the shoulder and underarm seams and the side seams, matching notches.

5 Leave an opening in the center back of the skirt and gather the upper edge, joining it at the bodice. Turn up the lower edge of the skirt as far as the notch for the hem.

6 Stitch the underarm sleeve seam, gather the upper edge and place the seam at the notch in the front of the "arm-size," and stitch to bodice. Join the collar to the neck as notched.

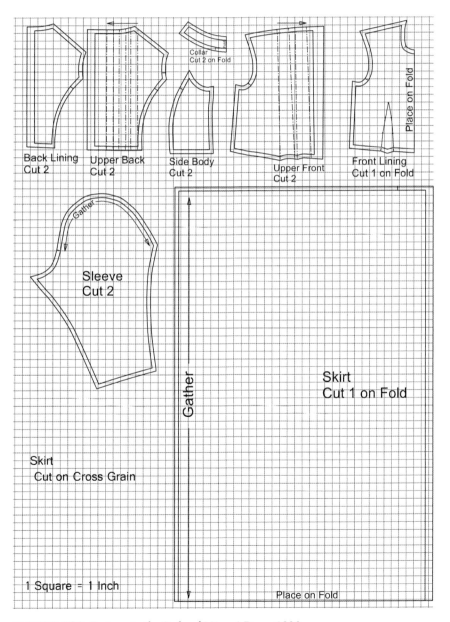

FIGURE 186 *Pattern in the Style of Misses' Dress 1890.*

Shirtwaist Waist 1912

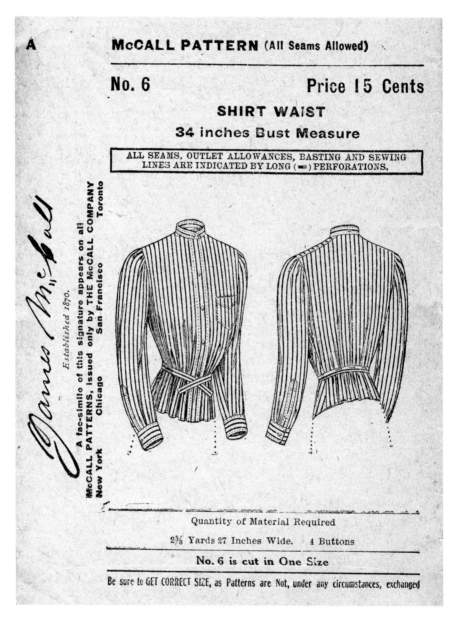

FIGURE 187 *Shirtwaist. McCall 6, 1912.10.JSE. Commercial Pattern Archive.*

34-inch bust: requires 2⅝ yards 27 inches wide; 24-inch waist: requires 4 yards 27 inches wide.
  Eight pieces: front, back, neckband, pocket, sleeve, cuff, facing, underlap.
  Match notches to close seams:

1 Right front—fold center front over 2 inches to right side, turn edge under, and topstitch in place.

2 Left front—fold center front under 1 inch to wrong side, turn edge, and topstitch for form underlap.

3 Stitch shoulder seams and side seams together.

4 Gather waistline to fit and sew a ¾-inch-wide stay belt over gathers in the inside to fasten in front.

5 Stitch neckband with right sides together; turn through lower edge; attach to neck, allowing for overlap at center front.

6 Pocket: turn upper edge over on outside and sew on left front with upper edges at small circles.

7 Stitch sleeve seam to lower notch, attach facing, and underlap to finish opening.

8 Gather top of sleeve to set into armhole, gather lower edge to fit cuff, and finish in same manner as neckband.

9 Hem shirtwaist.

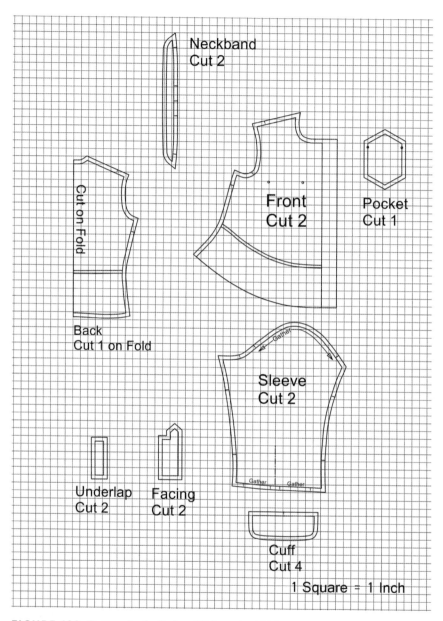

FIGURE 188 *Pattern in the Style of Shirtwaist 1912.*

Seven-Gored Skirt 1912

FIGURE 189 *Seven-Gored Skirt. McCall 7, 1912.11.JSE. Commercial Pattern Archive.*

Six pieces: center-front gore, side-front gore, side-back gore, center-back gore, placket facing, and belt.

Match notches to close seams: ½-inch seam allowance (original specifies 1-inch seam allowance at the shoulder and underarm for any alterations in fitting and ⅜ inch at neck and armhole).

1 Join center front to side front.

2 Join side front to side back.

3 Join side back to center back.

4 Stitch placket facing to center back above circle, right sides together; open and fold to create underlap.

5 Stitch belt to skirt with lap on left side of the back.

6 Hem to the appropriate length.

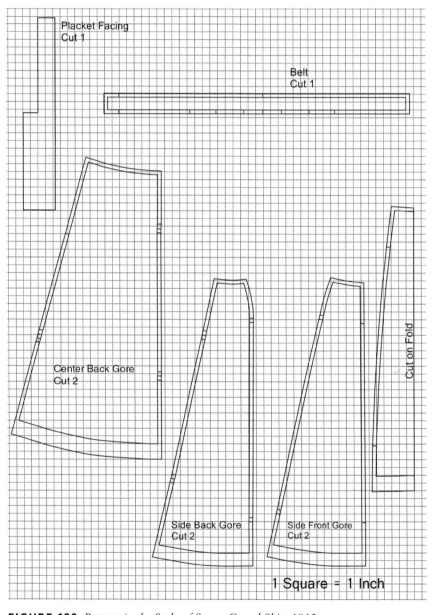

FIGURE 190 *Pattern in the Style of Seven-Gored Skirt 1912.*

Misses' and Women's One-Piece Frock 1929

FIGURE 191 *Misses' and Women's One-Piece Frock. Vogue 9656, 1929.104.JSE. Commercial Pattern Archive.*

Eighteen years: bust 36, hip 39; finished length at center back from natural neckline 41 inches. Requires 3¾ yards of 36-inch or 3⅜ yards of 39-inch material; 1¼ yards of 36-inch or 1 yard of 39-inch material for lining.

Eight pieces: lining front and back, frock front, blouse back, skirt back, sleeve, tie, and girdle.

1. Lining—stitch front darts at underarms; stitch shoulder seams, easing back to front; stitch side seams; pique neckline, armholes, and hem edges.

2. Blouse—dart blouse front at side. Make inside pin tuck on dash continuing from dart; make inside pin tucks below this on small dots. Make inside ⅛-inch tucks on dash line at back of neck. Stitch underarm seams and shoulder seams from neck to square, matching notches.

3. Stitch dart in frock front skirt; join skirt back to front. French seam or trim seams and overcast before pressing open.

4. Run five rows of shirring on lines across top back of skirt. Turn under seam allowance at lower edge of blouse. Adjust gathers and stitch blouse back over skirt.

5. Neck—finish neckline with narrow facing. Hem loose edges of tie to dots. Turn under seam allowance on end. Apply to front, matching markings, and stitch. Knot loose ends.

6. Sleeves—gather sleeve at wrist between notches. Gather to about 4 inches and fasten. Adjust and seam sleeve above notch, easing at elbow by matching notches. Finish

opening and lower edge of sleeve with ribbon seam binding. Work thread loops on back line of shirring, sew buttons to front line, lap, and fasten snugly at wrist. Turn under seam allowance at lower edge of kimono sleeve. Match marking and stitch over sleeve. Face kimono armhole when sleeveless.

7 Join frock to lining along crosswise dots.

8 Girdle—make inside ¼-inch tucks on front girdle as marked at dashed lines. Hem loose edges. Tie at center back, covering sewing.

9 Lower edge: allow frock to hang—various materials sag differently when cut circular— even off sag and turn up lower edge. Sew ribbon binding to edge of back skirt. Hem the binding to the skirt. Keep stitches loose, catching up only a thread or two to hold hem. Hem front of skirt as perforated.

10 Press each section thoroughly as the work progresses.

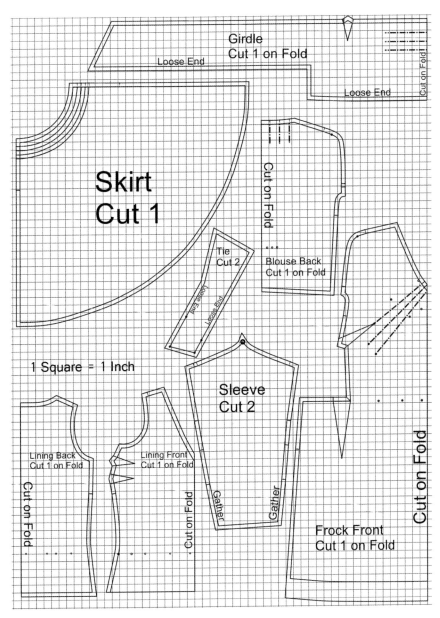

Girdle
Cut 1 on Fold

Loose End

Loose End

Cut on Fold

**Skirt
Cut 1**

Cut on Fold

Tie
Cut 2

Loose End

Loose End

Blouse Back
Cut 1 on Fold

1 Square = 1 Inch

**Sleeve
Cut 2**

Lining Back
Cut 1 on Fold

Lining Front
Cut 1 on Fold

Cut on Fold

Cut on Fold

Gather

Gather

Cut on Fold

**Frock Front
Cut 1 on Fold**

FIGURE 192 *Pattern in the Style of Misses' and Women's One-Piece Frock 1929.*

Misses' and Women's Blouse 1937

FIGURE 193 *Misses' and Women's Blouse. Simplicity 2389, 1937.29.JSE. Commercial Pattern Archive.*

Size 16: bust 34, waist 28, hip 39, neck to waist length 23 inches.

Requires 2⅞ yards for 35- or 39-inch material or 1¾ yards for 59-inch material.

Suggested fabrics: dimity, dotted swiss, sheer cotton, handkerchief linen, silk or rayon crepe, wool crepe, sheer woolens.

Seven pieces: blouse front and back, yoke front and back, collar, sleeve, and cuff.

Seam allowance: ½ inch for all seams; left side facing with 9-inch slide fastener (zipper).

1 Front keyhole opening: cut a facing 3 inches wide and 8 inches long, turn ¼ inch on side edges and one end, and stitch.

2 Baste facing to front of blouse with centers matching, and stitch down ¼ inch each side of center 6¾ inches from neckline; slash between stitching; turn facing inside and tack in place.

3 Gather blouse front and blouse back ½ inch and ⅝ inch from upper edges.

4 Turn in top edge of front yoke; join to Blouse Front pulling up gathers to fit and topstitch.

5 Repeat for the back yoke and blouse back; join shoulder seams.

6 Join the side seams, leaving the left side open between the notches; stitch front waist tucks.

7 Left side closing: baste seam opening, place at center of zipper, baste. Remove basting; pull slider down and stitch as far as possible; pull slider up and stitch other side, forming a point at each end.

8 Collar: stitch right sides together, turn. Baste to neck edge of blouse on outside, matching notches, finish neck edge with bias facing. Fasten upper end of keyhole opening with hook and eye.

9 Sleeve: gather at top and at wrist, stitch underarm seam, leaving 3-inch opening at wrist, finish, and add cuff finished at 1½ inch. Stitch sleeve in armhole.

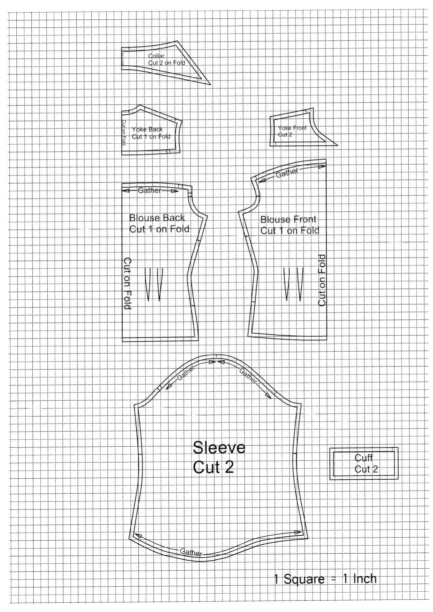

FIGURE 194 *Pattern in the Style of Misses' and Women's Blouse 1937.*

Misses' and Women's Slack-Suit 1942

FIGURE 195 *Misses' and Women's Slack-Suit or Coverall. Simplicity 4104, 1942.106.URI. Commercial Pattern Archive.*

Size 16: bust 34, waist 28, hips 37; finished back length from base of neck to waist, 16 inches; finished length from waist at side seam to lower edge of trousers, 41 inches.

Eight pieces: blouse front and back, collar, sleeve, trousers front and back, pocket, and belt.

Requires 4¼ yards of 35-inch material or 3¾ yards of 39-inch material.

Suggested fabrics: chambray, linen, piqué, seersucker, denim, rayon shantung.

Match notches to close seams, use flat-stitched seams when appropriate; ¾-inch seam allowance at underarm, ½-inch elsewhere. Center-front button and side slide fastener (zipper) closing (9-inch for left side closing) and button on drop-seat.

1   Stitch darts in front blouse and front trousers.

2   Make belt carriers: cut two strips each 2 inches by 5 inches, fold each in half lengthwise, and stitch, leaving ends open; turn and stitch along long edges. Fold each carrier in half and baste to loose edge of blouse front on outside over dart.

3   Join front blouse to front trousers, easing in fullness of blouse between notch and side seam, and turn seam downward; topstitch center-front seam.

4   Clip front trousers to seam allowance, join to front crotch seam.

5   Hem facings: fold center-front facing extensions to outside from fold to notch, stitch at neck, clip, and turn.

6   Front opening: Lap front opening edges, matching waist seam, stitch through all thicknesses at bottom of opening.

7   Trouser pockets: baste under ½ inch on all edges, turn hem to inside, stitch pockets to trouser fronts.

8   Blouse back: stitch darts; join center back, matching notches.

9   Join shoulder seams, matching notches, easing in back fullness.

10 Join sleeve to blouse, easing in the fullness between notches; stitch sleeve and blouse underarm seams to waist.

11 Collar: face, leaving notched edges open; turn and join to neck edge of blouse. Turn in free edge and slip-stitch over seam on outside. Topstitch outer edge of collar.

12 Trouser back: stitch darts, match notches, and stitch center back; join inner leg seam, matching crotch seams.

13 Back trouser facing: cut bias 3 inches wide. Stitch under ½ inch on one long edge. With right sides together, join bias to upper and side edges.

14 Side opening with zipper: turn back facing to inside and baste. Baste under arm seam allowances on opening edges. Place the edges at center of closed zipper with tab end at waistline; baste, turning in upper ends of tape. Stitch in place ¼ inch from edges.

15 Back closing: work buttonholes at top of trousers back, working center one a little to one side of seam. Stitch ½-inch-wide cotton tape across blouse back at waistline on inside at medium circles, sew buttons to blouse back.

16 Belt: fold and stitch, leaving an opening, turn and slip-stitch opening. Work buttonholes between small dots and at center back. Button belt in place, sew buckle to left end, and work eyelet on right.

17 Sleeve and trouser hems: turn up lower edge 1½ inch. Turn under raw edge and stitch flat.

18 Front closing: work buttonholes on right front, sew buttons under buttonholes, and hook at waistline.

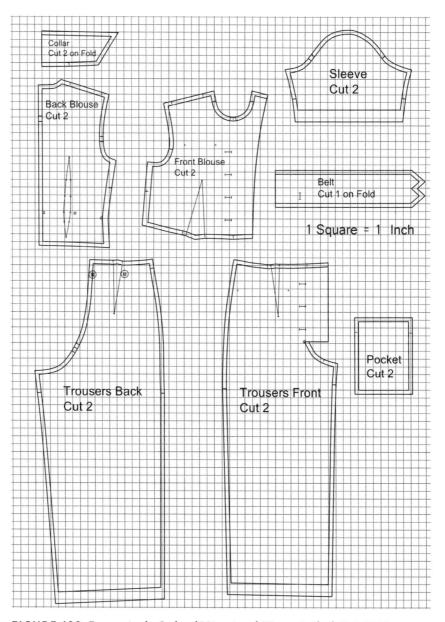

FIGURE 196 *Pattern in the Style of Misses' and Women's Slack-Suit 1942.*

Misses' Dress with Cowl Neckline 1952

FIGURE 197 *Misses' Dress with Cowl Neckline. Advance 6124, 1952.165.BWS. Commercial Pattern Archive.*

Size 18: bust 36, waist 30, hip 39, width across back 14½, finished length from center of shoulder over bust to natural waist 17¾, finished skirt side-front length from natural waistline 31, and 2-inch hem.

Requires 4⅝ yards of 35-inch, 4½ yards 39-inch or 4¼ yards 45-inch fabric (about ⅛ yard more if striped fabric).

Suggested materials: crepe, taffeta, shantung, lightweight wool, sheer cotton or rayon, novelty cotton or rayon.

Six pieces: bodice back and front, cowl, back neck facing, skirt, and belt.

Seam allowance: ½ inch for all seams; back closing with 20-inch slide fastener (zipper) [original pattern calls for a 10-inch zipper].

1   Stitch fitting darts in the bodice back and join the center-back seam from the neck to the large dot; leave the rest open for the placket.

2   Stay-stitch the front bodice neckline ⅜ inch from edge; stitch fitting darts.

3   Cowl: hem cowl ½ inch on unnotched edge. Pleat ends of cowl by bringing small perforations to meet medium perforations and baste. Join notched edge of cowl to neck edge of bodice, matching notches, and ease cowl between notches.

4   Join shoulder seams, matching notches. Place finished edge of cowl ½ inch below back of neck edge. Clip seam at end of cowl and press toward back.

5   Back neck facing: hem ½ inch on unnotched edge. Join to back neckline, matching notches, and allow facing to extend ½ inch beyond shoulder seam. Clip neck seam and turn facing inside. Slip-stitch ½ inch on shoulder edges of facing to seam.

6   Join side seams of bodice.

7   Skirt: box pleat to fit waist following arrows; join center back seam, leaving 3½-inch opening at waist for zipper.

8   Join waistline seam, keeping point of bodice at center-front pleat; clip skirt at center front. Turn and baste ½ inch on edges of center-back placket. Insert zipper in opening with edges meeting at center of teeth. Stitch close to teeth.

9   Cut 1½-inch strip of bias 1 inch longer than sleeve width. Join to outside of sleeve and turn to the inside. Turn ½ inch and fell-stitch to the sleeve.

10   Adjust dress to desired length and hem.

11   Belt: baste interfacing, fold in half lengthwise, right sides together, and seam one end and the long edge. Trim seams, trimming interfacing close to stitching, and turn. Turn in ½ inch on open end and blind-stitch. Attach buckle.

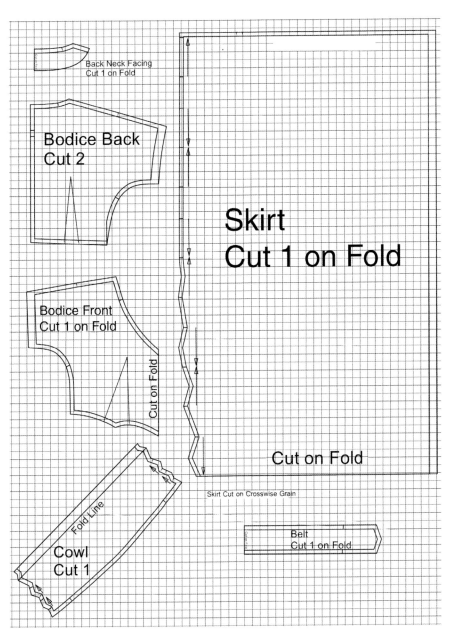

FIGURE 198 *Pattern in the Style of Misses' Dress with Cowl Neckline 1952.*

Nehru Jacket 1968

FIGURE 199 *Nehru Jacket. Spadea X-161, 1968.413.URI. Commercial Pattern Archive.*

Size 42: chest 42, waist 38, finished length (Style 1) 29½ inches with separating collar, (Style 2) 37 inches with pockets and closed collar.

Style 1 requires 3 yards of 45-inch-wide material, 2⅞ yards of 39-inch-wide lining, and 1 yard of 45-inch-wide interfacing; Style 2 requires 3½ yards 45-inch-wide material, 3⅛ yards 39-inch-wide lining, and 1¼ yards 45-inch-wide interfacing.

Suggested fabrics: heavy cotton, linen, corduroy, madras, synthetic leather, gabardine, flannel, raw silk.

Ten Pieces: jacket front, side front, side back, back, collar (longer style, shorter style), upper and under sleeve, jacket lining front, pocket (Style 2), and front interfacing. Cut two parts of interfacing for jacket front and collars; cut two of lining for jacket side front, side back, upper and under sleeve.

1   Join pocket to side seam of side back and side front (Style 2).

2   Join side backs to back, join side fronts to fronts; stitch dart in jacket back.

3   Join front and back at shoulder seam and side seam, including the pocket.

4 Catch-stitch the jacket front interfacing to the center front and baste to shoulder seam.

5 For separating smaller collar, turn the front self-facing outside, stitch from fold line to small *o*, clip, and turn facing to inside; for longer closed collar, stitch from fold line to medium *o*, clip, and turn facing to inside. Stay-stitch to the neckline.

6 Join the upper sleeve to the under sleeve and machine-gather to top of the sleeve between notches and ease into the armhole.

7 Hem sleeve and jacket.

8 Join jacket front lining to side back lining, then to back lining.

9 From outside, form soft pleat ½ inch deep at center back lining and catch-stitch horizontally at neckline and waistline.

10 Slip-stitch lining inside jacket, turning back ⅝ inch on lining edge; assemble sleeve lining and finish as jacket lining.

11 Interface collar using pad stitch, stitch upper collar to under collar, leaving neck edge open, and turn.

12 Join interfaced collar portions to jacket neck edge between small *o*'s for separating smaller collar, to medium *o*'s for closed longer collar. Clip curve. Turn free edge and slip-stitch on side of jacket.

13 Finish front with buttonholes and buttons; fasten closed collar with hooks and eyes.

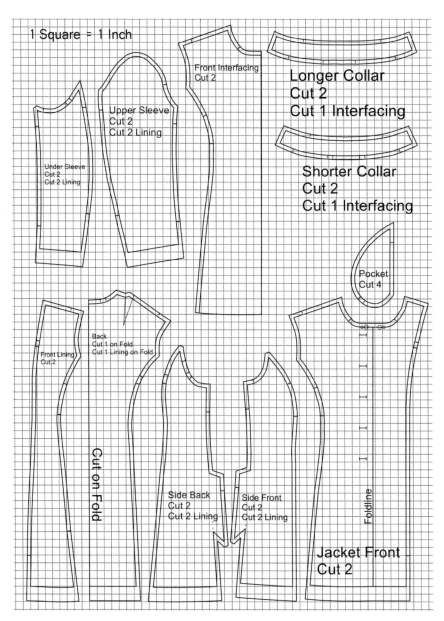

1 Square = 1 Inch

Front Interfacing
Cut 2

Longer Collar
Cut 2
Cut 1 Interfacing

Upper Sleeve
Cut 2
Cut 2 Lining

Shorter Collar
Cut 2
Cut 1 Interfacing

Under Sleeve
Cut 2
Cut 2 Lining

Pocket
Cut 4

Back
Cut 1 on Fold
Cut 1 Lining on Fold

Front Lining
Cut 2

Cut on Fold

Side Back
Cut 2
Cut 2 Lining

Side Front
Cut 2
Cut 2 Lining

Foldline

Jacket Front
Cut 2

FIGURE 200 *Pattern in the Style of Nehru Jacket 1968.*

Notes

Introduction

1. Numbers such as 1931.128.BWS indicate the date of issue, the number of patterns processed in the collection that year, and the initials indicate the collection.
2. A complete list can be found at http://copa.apps.uri.edu.
3. With references to material such as advertisements and patterns from magazine and catalog sources that span many years, specific in-text citations will include issue details corresponding to a generic entry provided for the magazine or catalog with title, publication details, and date range in the bibliography.

Chapter 2

1. Professional dressmakers or mantua makers were recognized by the eighteenth century. The profession was for women only to make mantuas, gowns worn over stays (corsets) and petticoats. The tradition of women being designated to make non-tailored garments was established at this time.
2. See Anonymous (1789).
3. See Lady (1808).
4. The title of *Godey's* varies: *Godey's Magazine, Lady's Book, Godey's Lady's Book*. For a biography of the editress Sara Josepha Hale, see Finley (1931).

Chapter 3

1. See Forsdyke (n.d.).

Chapter 4

1. Cut and punched patterns have a distinct advantage of small production costs for a limited number of patterns, say between twenty-five and one hundred. Cost for setting up the machinery to print the same number of patterns is considerable (Williams and Emery 1996).

Chapter 6

1. *Style*, published by American Fashion Company, should not be confused with another earlier magazine of the same name, published by Domestic Sewing Machine Company until it ceased operation by 1895. To further confuse matters, Style was an English pattern company, with its own publication, that started in the 1950s.

2. An English pattern company issued Economy Design patterns in the 1940s. An example circa 1941 in the Commercial Pattern Archive database is for the "Make-Do and Mend" campaign.

3. For a complete listing of English publishing corporations and pattern companies, see Seligman (1996: 302–307; 2003: 95–105).

4. For a brief history of home economics, see Helveston and Bubloz (1999).

5. *Vogue* in January 1918 featured society women in Hoover aprons (40), and the December issue featured society women in the uniform selling pies to support the war effort at the Ritz, Sherry's, Delmonico's, and the Plaza (25).

Chapter 7

1. It could be argued that Demorest printed the first patterns in the United States, since the pattern sheets given first in *Frank Leslie's Lady's Gazette of Fashion* and then in each issue of *Demorest's Monthly Magazine* had the outline of the pattern pieces printed on a sheet of tissue paper. In addition, it could be argued that the over-printed pattern sheets were "printed patterns." These, however, were not "printed" patterns. The Demorest patterns printed the outlines of pattern pieces with smaller pieces inside the larger pieces. If they were cut out to place on the fabric, it would leave major holes in half of the pattern pieces, which could, and probably did, cause distortion of the pattern. The over-printed sheets had to have each piece copied off by hand before they could be used.

2. McCall used French designers to strengthen their whole line. They did not usually identify the designers on the pattern envelope, only in the description of the pattern in *McCall's Magazine* and in catalogs. Williams notes the couturier patterns "all have something a little extra; that manner in which the skirt fullness is achieved, a clever way of manipulating a ruffle of diagonal seam to replace darts" (1995: 6).

3. Pattern companies continue this practice with all major international fashion events for the latest styles for new patterns.

4. During the 1920s, Butterick averaged 600–800 new styles per year; Standard averaged 400–500 a year until its takeover in 1926; and Ladies' Home Journal offered 350–450 Home pattern styles per year and produced 294 couturier patterns in 1929. Pictorial Review averaged 500–600 per year, McCall 450–500 per year, and Excella 300–400 per year. Vogue averaged 500 regular styles through the 1920s, 115 children's from 1925, and 100 Special Designs from 1929, for a total of 500–600 new styles per year. In addition, all issued a few needlework designs each year.

Chapter 8

1. The *Hollywood Pattern Book* was introduced in 1933 and included promotional photos from new films, articles about what the stars were wearing, and information about the designers, as well as

a catalog of new Hollywood patterns. The publication was retitled *Glamour of Hollywood* in 1939 and was shortened to *Glamour* in 1941. The magazine *Charm* was incorporated with *Glamour* in 1959, which is still in publication.

Chapter 9

1. Since L-85 restrictions were not imposed on the pattern companies, patch pockets were allowed.

2. Lend Lease, begun in March 1941, was the program under which the United States supplied the Allied nations with vast amounts of war matériel between 1941 and 1945.

Chapter 10

1. Even Hollywood was caught. The studios had films with pre–New Look styles in preparation; to play it safe until the new fashion was established, most of the film shots showed the stars only from the waist up.

2. The main pattern types fall into five categories: girls/boys, teen, junior, miss, and women. Girls/boys are generally sizes 7–14 with an average height of about five feet. Teens are generally sizes 10–16 with an average height of five feet, three inches. Juniors are generally sizes 11–17 with an average height of five feet, five inches. Misses are generally sizes 12–20 with an average height of five feet, six inches. Women are generally sizes 40–50 with an average height of five feet, six inches and are based on the bust measurement. The companies began to offer half-size patterns in the mid-1940s for women five feet, three inches and under. Men's sizes were based on chest measurements of thirty-two to fifty inches.

Chapter 11

1. Stretch and Sew Inc. (n.d.), "Patterns, Books & Notions," https://www.gmidesign.com/stretch/, accessed March 10, 2011.

2. Folkwear Sewing Patterns (n.d.), "About Folkwear," http://www.folkwear.com/aboutfolkwear.html, accessed March 10, 2011.

3. Simplicity has produced a line of Daisy Kingdom patterns for infants and toddlers since the late 1980s that has no relationship to the Daisy Kingdom Pattern Company.

Chapter 12

1. Sergers had been around for over 100 years for industrial use. The inventors, J. Maken Merrow and his son Joseph, patented a machine for crochet stitching in 1881, which led to the development of the overlock machine. The stitches allow for the stretch in various knit fabrics and overcast the edge of the fabric to prevent fraying. The machines are known as merrows, overlocks, or sergers.

2. Rev. Sun Myung Moon, Korean founder and leader of the worldwide Unification Church, is famous for holding blessing ceremonies, often referred to as "mass weddings." It is reported that 4,000 couples were married in Seoul, South Korea, in 2000.

3. *Project Runway*, a reality TV show that first aired in the United States in December 2004, was in its ninth season in 2011. Contestants compete with each other to design and produce the best clothes.

Bibliography

Primary Sources

Advance Complete Counter Catalog (1935), New York: Advance Pattern Co.

Alcega, J. de ([1580] 1979), *Libro de geometria practia y traca (Book of the Practice of Tailoring Measuring and Marking Out)*, facsimile of 1589 edition with introduction by Jean Pain and Celia Brainton, Carlton, Bedford: Ruth Bean Publications.

American Fabrics (1967), "The U.S. Home Sewing Circle—41,000,000 Strong," 76 (Summer): 65.

Anonymous (1789), *Instructions for Cutting out Apparel for the Poor; Principally Intended for the Assistance of the Patronesses of Sunday Schools and Other Charitable Institutions, but Useful in all Families. Containing Patterns, Directions, and Calculations, Whereby the Most Inexperienced May Readily Buy Materials, Cut Out and Value Each Article of Clothing of Every Size, Without the Least Difficulty, and With the Greatest Exactness: With a Preface, Containing a Plan for Assisting the Parents of Poor Children Belonging to Sunday Schools, to Clothe Them, and Other Official Observations*, London: J. Walters.

Arthur's Home Magazine (1866–1871), Philadelphia: T. S. Arthur & Co.

Athavaley, A. (2011), "A Stitch in Time . . . at the Speed of Smartphones," *Wall Street Journal* (May 12): D1.

Barron's (1958), "Profitable Patterns" (April 29): 9.

Barron's (1962), "Dirndls, Sheaths & Shifts" (July 23): 11.

Bendel, P. (1987a), "Market-Savvy Gyde: Keeping Simplicity on Target," *Sew News* (September): 42.

Bendel, P. (1987b), "Designer Ease, Pattern Company Licensees," *Sew News* (October): 33.

Blacker, M. (1943), "Fashions in 1943," *Journal of Home Economics*, 35/2 (February): 73–77.

Le Bon Ton (1867), New York: S. T. Taylor, 16 (January): 1.

Book of Fashions (1918), New York: McCall Pattern Co., VI/1 (Spring): 4.

Business Week (1935), "Dress Pattern Progress" (February 16): 20.

Business Week (1942), "Susie Sews" (June 13): 58.

Business Week (1943), "Sewing Success" (March 13): 68, 71.

Butterick Catalogs (ca. 1869–Spring 1871), New York: Butterick Publishing Co.

Catalog of the Bazar Paper Patterns (1871), New York: McCall Pattern Co.

Catalogue of Domestic Paper Fashions (1875), New York: Domestic Sewing Machine Co.: 31.

Chatzky, J. (1992), "Reaping from Sewing," *Forbes*, 149/11 (May 25): 154.

Clandenning, A. (2001), "Checkered Future for Sewing Patterns," *Times Union, Albany* (3 June), www.timesunion.com, accessed September 14, 2012.

Cook and Golding, J. (1815), *The Tailor's Assistant; or, Unerring Instructor: Containing an Analysis of The Art of Cutting, To Fit The Human Form With Ease and Elegance, Upon True Scientific Principles, Or Geometrical Proportions*, London: J. Rash.

Le Costume Royal (1918), New York: Royal Pattern Co., V23/3 (December): 3.

Delineator (1873–1937), New York: Butterick Publishing Co.

Demorest (1877), *Catalogue of Demorest Reliable Patterns,* New York: W.J. Demorest.

Demorest's Monthly Magazine (1860–1889), New York: W. J. Demorest.

Designer (1894–1920), New York: Standard Fashion.

Devere, L. ([1866] 1986), *The Handbook of Practical Cutting on the Centre Point System*, reprint, Lopez Island, WA: R. L. Shep.

Elite Styles (1918), New York: Elite Styles Co.

Forbes (1971), "I Made It Myself" (April 15): 43.

Frank Leslie's Lady's Gazette of Fashion (January 1854–September 1856), New York: Frank Leslie.

Greene, J. (1967), "Affluent Sew-ciety," *Barron's* (August 21): 11, 19.

Giles, E. ([1887] 1987), *The History of the Art of Cutting in England*, London: F.T. Prewett; Reprint, Lopez Island, WA: R.L. Shep.

Godey's Ladies' Book (September 1851–February 1854), Philadelphia.

Golding, J. (1817), *Golding's New Edition of the Tailor's Assistant or Improved Instructor*, Part I, London: F. Mason.

Golding, J. (1818), *Golding's New Edition of the Tailor's Assistant or Improved Instructor,* Part II, London: F. Mason.

Harper's Bazar (1867–1913), New York: Harper & Brothers.

Hobby, E. (1964), "Casual Fashions Appeal to Home Sewers," *Barron's* (December 7): 9–10.

Hollywood Pattern Book (1935), New York: Hollywood Pattern Co. (April/May).

Howard, T. (1962), "High Fashion for Housewives," *Saturday Evening Post* reprint. Commercial Pattern Archive, University of Rhode Island: 34–36.

Ideas for Sewing with Cotton Bags (1955), Memphis, TN: National Cotton Council.

Journal des Demoiselles (1833–1911), Paris: Bureau du Journal.

Ladies' Home Journal (1905–1930), Philadelphia: Curtis Publishing Co.

The Ladies' Self Instructor in Millinery & Mantua Making, Embroidery & Appliqué ([1853] 1988), Philadelphia: Leary & Getz. Reprinted with additional illustrations from *Godey's Ladies' Book*, Mendocino, CA: R.L. Shep.

Ladies' World (1893), New York: S.H. Moore. (February): 12.

Lady, A [pseud.] (1808), *The Lady's Economical Assistant, or the Art of Cutting Out, and Making, the Most Useful Articles of Wearing Apparel, Without Waste; Explained by the Clearest Directions, and Numerous Engravings, of Appropriate and Tasteful Patterns*, London: John Murray.

Lady, A [pseud.] (1838), *The Workwoman's Guide*, London: Simpkin, Marshall.

Lady's Companion (1925), London: George Newnes Ltd. (June): 142–63.

Lemontree, R. (1983), "What Does 'Easy' Really Mean?," *Sew News* (August/September): 33.

Life Magazine (1943), "Life's Dress, Hattie Carnegie Designed It For Home Sewing" (April 12): 51–53.

Life Magazine (1947), "Skirts: Up or Down?" (May 12): 99.

Life Magazine (1970), "The Midi Muscles In" (August 21): 24–27.

Make and Mend for Victory (1942), n.p.: Spool Cotton Co.

McCall's Magazine (1879–1974), New York: McCall Co.

McCall Pattern Co. (1943), "The Pattern Industry's Place in the War-Time Economy," unpublished manuscript. Emery Papers, *Pattern Companies*, Box 2, Commercial Pattern Archive, University of Rhode Island.

Merwin, P. (1908), *The American System of Dressmaking*, Kansas City, MO: American College of Dressmaking.

Metropolitan Monthly (1871), New York: Butterick Publishing Co. (May).

Microsystems Technology (n.d.), "Simplicity Pattern Cuts a New, Sleeker Shape with OCR for Forms™," article photocopy. Williams Papers, *Dressmaking History, Series V*, Box 3, University of Rhode Island.

Miller, S. (2012), "Sew Independent" *Threads*, Newtown, CT: Taunton Press (October/November): 64–68.

Minister's Gazette of Fashion (1853), editorial insert, London: Minister & Co. (September): 23.

Minister, Edward ([1853] 1993), *The Complete Guide to Practical Cutting*, reprint, Mendocino, CA: R.L. Shep.

Mitchell, J. (ed.) (1883), *American Tailor and Cutter*, New York: John J. Mitchell & Co. (July), 5/1: iii.

Molloy, J. (1975), *Dress for Success*, New York: Warner Books.

Molloy, J. (1977), *The Women's Dress for Success Book*, New York: Warner Books.

Moody's Manual of Investments: American and Foreign (1936–1946), New York: Moody's Investors Service.

New York Times (1941), (April 14).

Niles (MI) Daily Star (1930), "New Factory of Niles" (August 26): front page.

Penny, V. ([1863] 1996), *The Employments of Women: A Cylopedia of Women's Work*, reprint edition, n.p.: Mrs. Martins Mercantile and Millinery.

Peterson's Magazine (January 1857–December 1879), Philadelphia.

Petit Courrier des Dames (1842–1847), Paris: Imp. de V. Dondey-Dupré.

Picken, M. (1921), *Tissue-Paper Pattern*, Parts 1 and 2, Scranton, PA: Women's Institute of Domestic Arts & Science.

Pictorial Review (1900–1939), New York: Pictorial Review Co.

Pictorial Review (1922), "Pictograf No. 2810," New York: Pictorial Review Co.

Queen, J., and Lapsley, W. (1809), *The Tailors' Instructor*, Philadelphia: J. Queen and W. Lapsely.

Read, B., Buck, A., Hyde, R., and Saunders, A. (1984), "Benjamin Read's Splendid Views: Six Topographical Prints Showing Winter and Summer Fashions: Taken From The Hand-Coloured Aquatints, 1829–1839," London: Guildhall Library and the Costume Society.

Rutberg, S. (1993), "Bottom Line," *Women's Wear Daily* (February 8): 12.

Scott, G. (1840), advertising flyer. Williams Papers, *Dressmaking History, Series V,* Box 1, University of Rhode Island.

Scott, G. (1849), *Scott's Mirror of Fashion* (January 1), XI/3: 4.

Smart Clothes for Fall and Winter (1934), New York: Singer Sewing Book.

Thorton, J. P. (1899), "Tailors of the Century," monthly feature, *Minister's Gazette of Fashions* (January–August).

Toilettes (1897), New York: Toilettes Publishing Co. (August): 26.

Vincent, W.D.F. (1890), *Cutter's Practical Guide To Cutting Every Kind of Garment Made By Tailors, In A Series of Parts*, London: Williamson Co. Ltd.

Vogue (1918), New York: Condé Nast (January, December).

Vogue (1922), "Instruction Sheet No. 6859," New York: Condé Nast.

Vogue Patterns (1998), "Vintage Vogue" (September/October): 23–27.

Weldon's Ladies' Journal (1920), London: Weldon's Ltd. (March): 1–48.

What the Woman's Institute Means to Me (1921), Scranton, PA: Women's Institute of Domestic Arts & Sciences.

Williamson, J. (ed.) (1873), *The Tailor and Cutter*, 9 (October 3).

The World of Fashion, Monthly Magazine, of the Courts of London and Paris (1836), London (October).

The World of Fashion, Monthly Magazine, of the Courts of London and Paris (1850), London (August).

Wright, G. (1894), "The Art of Cutting by Block Patterns," *West End Gazette* (September): 114.

Secondary Sources

Adburgham, A. (1989), *Shops and Shopping*, 2nd ed., London: Barrie & Jenkins.

Arnold, J. (1972), *Patterns of Fashion 1660–1860*, London: Macmillan.

Dickson, C.A. (1979), "Patterns for Garments: A History of the Paper Garment Pattern Industry in America to 1976," PhD dissertation, The Ohio State University.

Emery, J. (1997–1998), "Dating Vogue Designer Patterns 1958–1988," *Cutter's Research Journal*, 9/3 (Winter): 1, 5.

Emery, J. (1999), "Dreams on Paper," in B. Burman (ed.), *The Culture of Sewing*, Oxford: Berg, 235–53.

Emery, J. (2001), "Dress Like a Star: Hollywood and the Pattern Industry," *Dress*, 28: 92–99.

Finley, R. E. (1931), *The Lady of Godey's, Sarah Josepha Hale*, Philadelphia, London: J. B. Lippincott Co.

Forsdyke, G. (n.d.), "A Brief History of the Sewing Machine," International Sewing Machine Collectors' Society, www.ismacs.net/sewing_machine_history.html, accessed February 10, 2010.

Heavens, S. (ed.) (2003), *Patterns* [catalog], Antwerp: MoMu, in association with Ludion.

Helveston, S., and Bubloz, M. (1999), "Home Economics & Home Sewing in the United States 1970–1940," in B. Burman (ed.), *The Culture of Sewing*, Oxford: Berg Press, 303–25.

"History of McCall's Pattern Co." (ca. 1994), unpublished manuscript. Emery Papers, *Pattern Companies*, Box 1, Commercial Pattern Archive, University of Rhode Island.

Kidwell, C. (1979), *Cutting a Fashionable Fit*, Washington, D.C.: Smithsonian Institution Press.

Kidwell, C., and Christman, M. (1974), *Suiting Everyone*, Washington, D.C.: Smithsonian Institution Press.

Lingeman, R. (1970), *Don't You Know There's a War On?* New York: G. P. Putnam's Sons.

McDermott, Kathleen (1993), "From 'Old Lady' to Industry Leader: Butterick, 1960–1992," unpublished manuscript. Emery Papers, *Pattern Companies*, Box 1, Commercial Pattern Archive, University of Rhode Island.

McDowell, C. (1997), *Forties Fashion*, London: Bloomsbury.

Mott, F. (1938), *A History of American Magazines*, vols 3–5, Cambridge, MA: Harvard University Press.

Paoletti, J. (1980), "The Role of Choice in the Democratization of Fashion," *Dress* 5/1: 47–56.

Peterson, T. (1964), *Magazines in the Twentieth Century*, Urbana: University of Illinois Press.

Reynolds, H. (1999), "'Your Clothes are the Materials of War': The British Government Promotion of Home Sewing during the Second World War," in B. Burman (ed.), *The Culture of Sewing*, Oxford: Berg, 327–39.

Rockwell, D. (attributed) (ca. 1964), "History of Butterick Pattern Company," unpublished manuscript. Emery Papers, *Pattern Companies*, Box 1, Commercial Pattern Archive, University of Rhode Island.

Ross, I. (1963), *Crusades and Crinolines*, New York: Harper and Row.

Seebohm, C. (1982), *The Man Who Was Called Vogue*, New York: Viking Press.

Seligman, K. L. (1996), *Cutting for All! The Sartorial Arts, Related Crafts, and Commercial Paper Pattern*, Carbondale and Edwardsville: Southern University Press.

Seligman, K. L. (2003), "Dressmaker Patterns: The English Commercial Pattern Industry 1878–1950," *Costume*, 37: 95–113.

Simplicity Pattern Company (1992), "Simplicity Pattern Company Chronology of Product and Events," unpublished manuscript. Emery Papers, *Pattern Companies*, Box 2, Commercial Pattern Archive, University of Rhode Island.

Simplicity Pattern Company (n.d.), "Simplicity Overview," unpublished manuscript. Emery Papers, *Pattern Companies*, Box 2, Commercial Pattern Archive, University of Rhode Island.

Tebbel, J., and Zuckerman, M. E. (1991), *The Magazine in America 1741–1990*, New York: Oxford University Press.

Trautman, P.A. (1987), *Clothing America*, New York: Costume Society of America.

Walsh, M. (1979), "The Democratization of Fashion: The Emergence of the Women's Dress Pattern Industry," *The Journal of American History* 66/2 (September): 299–313.

Williams, B. (1995), "1920s Couturier Patterns and the Home Sewer," *Cutters' Research Journal*, 6/4 (Spring): 1, 6–7.

Williams, B. (1996), "On the Dating of Tissue Paper Patterns, Part 1." *Cutters' Research Journal*, 8/2 (Fall): 2–10.

Williams, B. (1996–1997), "On the Dating of Tissue Paper Patterns, Part 2." *Cutters' Research Journal*, 8/3 (Winter): 2–10.

Williams, B., and Emery, J. (1996), Personal interview with Daniel Flint, owner, Famous Features Pattern Syndicate, New York City.

Archival Collections

Emery Papers, *Pattern Companies Papers*, Boxes 1–4, Emery Collection, Commercial Pattern Archive, Robert R. Carothers Libraries and Learning Commons, Special Collections, University of Rhode Island.

Williams Papers. *Dressmaking History, Series V*, Box 1, Betty Williams Collection, Robert R. Carothers Libraries and Learning Commons, Special Collections, University of Rhode Island.

Index